WHY
YOU
CAN
BUILD
IT
LIKE
THAT

WHY
YOU
CAN
BUILD
IT
LIKE
THAT

MODERN
ARCHITECTURE
EXPLAINED

 Thames & Hudson

John Zukowsky

CONTENTS

CHAPTER ONE
TRIUMPH OF GEOMETRY
8

CHAPTER TWO
SPACE AGE
52

INTRODUCTION
JOHN ZUKOWSKY

Two millennia ago Roman architect and civil engineer Vitruvius produced his architectural treatise titled *De Architectura* (*On Architecture*), in which he discussed not only the practicalities of architecture—urban planning, materials, machinery, for example—but also its social relevance. He wrote that architecture should embody '*firmitas, utilitas, venustas*', which has generally been translated as structural solidity and durability, utility or usefulness, and beauty or aesthetic impact. Although the act of 'building' connotes structure and utility, architecture also has an important visual component, and buildings throughout the centuries have either succeeded or failed in terms of both societal and individual aesthetic standards.

This book provides bold, eye-catching and distinctively striking examples of all three Vitruvian characteristics, rolled into one hundred extraordinary buildings created over the past seven decades. Not intended to be comprehensive, this worldwide selection discusses the work of a diverse range of architects from heroic early modernists, such as Ludwig Mies van der Rohe and Frank Lloyd Wright, to long-established firms such as Skidmore, Owings & Merrill. It also features mavericks of the past and present—Bruce Goff, Shin Takamatsu and Shigeru Ban—and singular architectural wonders that reflect their own times. What also links these, and all architectural projects, is the client–architect relationship. Unlike painters and some sculptors, who can create tangible expressions of art without a client, architects need clients to realize their dreams. The key to many of the buildings showcased within this book is that the architect–client dialogue was a productive one.

This volume contains a superb selection of buildings that reflect salient design characteristics. In chapter one—Triumph of Geometry—Mies's Lake Shore Drive (1951) is discussed as an early example of the gridded steel-and-glass high-rises that are commonplace today, and the Lotus Temple (1986) by Fariborz Sahba articulates the way in which geometry underlies natural forms. Although geometry and arithmetic calculation were used back through antiquity to design buildings, in the 20th century many architects boldly displayed the geometric basis of their designs for all to see. Chapter two—Space Age—highlights how influential technological developments such as jet-propelled air travel and ballistic missiles shaped postwar design expressions.

Curvilinear, anthropomorphic design made its way into architecture, and the space race between the Soviet Union and the United States fuelled even wilder designs and continued material experimentation. Not only was the space age memorialized, but the 21st century witnessed the construction of the first commercial spaceports, such as Spaceport America (2014) by Norman Foster.

The buildings that feature in chapter three—Making a Statement—are perhaps some of the most surprising designs in the book: unconventional and bizarre—Luxor Hotel (1993) and the 'Basket' headquarters (1997)—yet epitomizing successful client–architect relationships. Moreover, they relate to popular culture. Who cannot recognize the staggering impact of Disney and McDonald's across all social strata and international borders? Examples here, and throughout the book, project the image of what modern architecture is to the general public. Although all the buildings in chapter four—Skyscraper Style—are skyscrapers, each has its own distinct architectural form, defining its city and serving as a local landmark much as cathedrals did in European cities during the Middle Ages. These super-tall buildings are cities within a city, connecting to services and transport systems, and although skyscrapers are considered to be the most American of building types, today's giant of all giants is in the United Arab Emirates: Burj Khalifa (2010).

The final chapter—Homage to the Past—offers visual proof of the adage 'what goes around comes around'. The great historic industrial form of buildings such as Horno 3 Steel Museum (2007) demonstrates the persistence of history in determining their appearance, whereas designs such as Piazza d'Italia (1978) in New Orleans and the Jewish Museum (2001) in Berlin show the architect's creative interpretation of historic forms and events.

Above all, this book celebrates architects and buildings that pushed the boundaries of what was architecturally acceptable at the time they were built. Outlandish, innovative, controversial or simply unexpected, each design is one of a kind, yet each building reaffirms the Vitruvian values of '*firmitas, utilitas, venustas*' as much as its predecessors did. All these examples of modern architecture represent the art of architecture, as well as the art of the deal: the architect and client relationship that makes design a reality.

GUIDE TO SYMBOLS

Explains why the building is an important work of architecture.

Describes the architect's materials and techniques.

Locates the building in its historic and architectural context.

Unattributed quotes are by the architect featured.

Provides additional incidental information.

Lists examples of similar building designs.

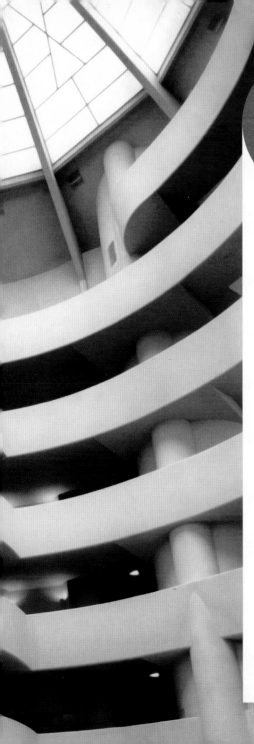

CHAPTER ONE
TRIUMPH OF GEOMETRY

Geometry has been used to plan buildings since antiquity in Islamic, ancient Greek, Egyptian and Roman architecture, for example. Often these simple planning shapes were hidden beneath a profusion of ornamentation, but the advent of European modernism during the interwar years of the 20th century stripped designs bare. The post-World War II era witnessed an international celebration of a building's geometry, and the designs in this chapter clearly demonstrate this, from the gridded rectangular planning of works by Ludwig Mies van der Rohe and Aldo Rossi, via the circular forms of Frank Lloyd Wright to giant cubes by Thom Mayne, A-frame triangles by Walter Netsch and Shigeru Ban, and even a trapezoid by I. M. Pei.

❮ Guggenheim Museum, New York City, New York, USA

Developer Herbert Greenwald equally deserves credit for the success of 860–880 because it was his vision to seek a new type of housing appropriate to postwar society. The Lake Shore Drive high-rises influenced the adoption of corporate modernism for residential structures in later buildings not only by Mies, but also by his own architectural disciples and students, and even by his competitors.

860–880 LAKE SHORE DRIVE

LUDWIG MIES VAN DER ROHE

1951

Gridded steel-and-glass, residential and commercial high-rises are commonplace today. However, when German émigré Ludwig Mies van der Rohe (1886–1969) designed these buildings at 860–880 Lake Shore Drive in Chicago, Illinois, they were revolutionary indeed. This is especially apparent when they are compared with the classically detailed masonry apartment buildings from the 1920s and 1930s situated around the corner along luxurious East Lake Shore Drive. Although Mies dreamed of building glass skyscrapers in Berlin during the 1920s, his actual works were often smaller stucco or brick-and-glass residences that were beautifully proportioned and detailed. Historians have said that his style changed after he moved to Chicago in 1938, to include more open spaces within his buildings and more open wall planes. He used large glass panes that further minimized the steel or concrete structural members, making tangible his oft-repeated 'less is more' mantra. Frank Lloyd Wright derided Mies's buildings such as 860–880 as 'flat-chested architecture'. Yet these twenty-six-storey residential towers, each 284 feet (86 m) high, spaced diagonally in a plaza, became beacons of their kind and were emulated across the globe. Krueck and Sexton restored the protected buildings in 2010.

Mies covered the structural steel with black painted steel, thereby lowering costs compared with masonry cladding. The construction price was $10.38 per square foot, comparable to the $8.55 of Mies's concrete-framed Promontory Apartments (1949). He refined the design into an independent glass and aluminium curtain wall at the adjacent Esplanade Apartments, 900–910 Lake Shore Drive (1955). This became commonplace for high-rise towers thereafter.

[Greenwald] began with an idea of social consequences of his work; along the way he also discovered that he was a very good businessman.

The Great Depression of the 1930s and World War II saw the rise of large planning teams, which continued after the war. Here, Mies was the design architect but former student Charles Genther of Pace Associates created the working drawings, and Holsman, Holsman, Klekamp and Taylor—specialists in apartment houses—critiqued the drawings.

Lafayette Park, 1956,
Ludwig Mies van der Rohe
Detroit, MI, USA

Westmount Square, 1967,
Ludwig Mies van der Rohe
Montreal, Canada

? The dynamic spaces of Wright's spiral-ramped art museum were intended to interact with the modern art on display. He locked horns with museum executives on the less than neutral interior and his desire for natural rather than artificial lighting, as well as the colour scheme. Their preferences were for a harsh museum white, whereas his choice leaned towards a warmer ivory tone. Nevertheless, the Guggenheim's distinct form influenced a number of museums, from Munich to Atlanta.

The spiral design was a natural for concrete construction. Wright stated: 'Concrete is a plastic material—susceptible to the impress of imagination.' In practical terms, it was less expensive than the stone construction he had preferred initially for his intended $2 million museum. (It cost considerably more when finished.)

GUGGENHEIM MUSEUM
FRANK LLOYD WRIGHT
1959

The Guggenheim Museum is the mid-century modern masterpiece of Frank Lloyd Wright (1867–1959), an icon equal to his modernist Fallingwater (1936–1939) and Prairie School Robie House (1910). Wright began the design in 1943 when modern art collector Solomon R. Guggenheim commissioned the museum. The spiral design was based on Wright's concept for the Gordon Strong Automobile Objective (1924) planned for Sugarloaf Mountain in Maryland. Even though Wright objected to highly urbanized New York City for the museum, several sites were investigated before the final one was selected in 1944, opposite Central Park. The model was unveiled in 1945, but construction was slow because Guggenheim had qualms about the nonconformist museum space and there were objections from civic groups. Even today many boldly designed buildings in New York face challenges from vocal neighbourhood associations and city commissions. Some of them protested against the Gwathmey Siegel Kaufman additions to the museum in 1992 even though they completed Wright's original ideas. In 2008 the museum's signature atrium and skylight were restored by WASA Studio and a team of specialists.

BMW Museum,
1973, Karl
Schwanzer
Munich, Germany

*The High Museum
of Art,* 1983,
Richard Meier
Atlanta, GA, USA

The open rectilinear spaces of Wright's Prairie School buildings responded to the rambling hills of his native Wisconsin. But circular forms can be seen in designs such as the second Jacobs House (1948) in Middleton, Wisconsin, 140 Maiden Lane (1948), San Francisco, and the David Wright House (1952), Phoenix.

The design features Mediterranean-style vaults of terracotta and brick walls, in part because the U.S. embargo of 1960 inhibited the use of steel-reinforced concrete. With the Cuban Missile Crisis of 1962 redirecting that country's spending towards defence, the schools were not considered a priority within the national budget, and the complex remains unfinished.

NATIONAL ART SCHOOLS

PORRO, GOTTARDI AND GARATTI

1961

These dramatically domed, intertwined, organic architectural forms are a tangible result of the Cuban Revolution of 1959. The five National Art Schools in Havana—for modern dance, arts, drama, music and ballet—were designed by three architects, but their foundation is credited to Fidel Castro and Che Guevara as a way to reform public education. Built on the site of a former country club in an affluent neighbourhood, they are the work of Cuban-born and Havana- and Paris-trained Ricardo Porro (1925–), with Italians Roberto Gottardi and Vittorio Garatti (both 1927–). Porro designed the schools of Modern Dance (shown here) and Plastic Arts, whereas Gottardi designed the school of Dramatic Arts, and Garatti the schools of Music and Ballet. Together, the team created a distinct educational complex that became architecturally controversial when Soviet rectilinear functionalism became the norm a few years later. This influenced its lack of completion, decline in use, and criticism of its bourgeois elitism; it also fuelled the political exile of Porro and Garatti. The almost archaeological complex within jungle overgrowth achieved increased recognition in the 1980s and 1990s, and inclusion within UNESCO's World Heritage list in 2003 and Cuba's national landmark inventory in 2010.

Catalan vaults are similar to Guastavino tiled vaults, patented in 1885 by Spanish-born Rafael Guastavino. Contemporary architects such as Map13 use computer programs to make dynamically expressive thin-tiled structures.

The designers aimed to create a new Cuban national architecture, which would relate to Che Guevara's idea of building an experimental free school devoted to the arts for this new post-revolutionary age. The vaulted design and interconnected spaces were intended to combine the best modern organic design of the era, such as that practised by Alvar Aalto and Frank Lloyd Wright, with native traditions and Hispanic influences, witnessed in its Catalan vaults in particular.

Mapungubwe National Park Interpretive Centre, 2009, Michael Ramage, John Ochsendorf, Peter Rich, James Bellamy and Philippe Block
South Africa

Crossway Eco-Home, 2012, Richard Hawkes
near Staplehurst, Kent, UK

Bricktopia Pavilion, 2013, Map13
Barcelona, Spain

? Observatory architecture has traditionally been domed or globe-shaped. Even a dynamic example such as Erich Mendelsohn's Einstein Tower (1924) in Potsdam, Germany, has a dome. Goldsmith's angular solution to this building type is an aesthetic one that was based on engineering practicality. He stated it was 'Miesian' in its simplicity, form and functionality: 'Architecture out of the fact, the plan, the planning limitations, the limitations of normal structures.' It set the tone for recent observatories that are more individually functional.

Yerkes Observatory, 1897, Henry Ives Cobb
Williams Bay, WI, USA

Griffith Park Observatory, 1935, J.C. Austin and Frederick Ashley
Los Angeles, CA, USA

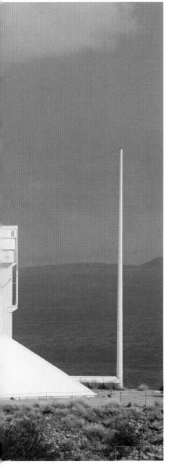

**McMATH-PIERCE
SOLAR TELESCOPE**
MYRON GOLDSMITH
1962

The unassuming, contemplative Myron Goldsmith (1918–1996) was one of the design partners in Chicago's massive office of Skidmore, Owings & Merrill (SOM). Goldsmith trained as an architect and engineer, and worked briefly in the office of Ludwig Mies van der Rohe from 1946 to 1953 before embarking on a study fellowship with Italian engineer and architect Pier Luigi Nervi from 1953 to 1955. Goldsmith then took a position with the San Francisco office of SOM from 1955 to 1958, where he joked about 'being a structural engineer in a high-risk seismic zone'. From there he relocated to the Chicago office, where he became a partner in 1967. Goldsmith designed several telescopes in the United States and Chile. The most striking of these is McMath-Pierce Solar Telescope at the National Observatory atop Kitt Peak outside Tucson, Arizona, at a height of 6,880 feet (2,097 m). Of this notably modern solar telescope, President John F. Kennedy wrote that it was '. . . a source of pride to our nation' as the 'largest instrument for solar research in the world'. It still is the world's largest solar telescope, although a larger one, not yet operational but under construction, will be the Daniel K. Inouye Solar Telescope in Maui, Hawaii.

Goldsmith created well-proportioned, minimalist buildings such as the Republic Newspaper (1971), Columbus, Indiana, and clever solutions like the cantilevered hangars at San Francisco International Airport (1958; demolished).

The white painted steel structure contains a 110-foot-high (33-m) tower that merges with a 500-foot (152-m) diagonal shaft, which penetrates the ground. Its 32-degree angle is intended to parallel the Earth's axial rotation, thereby enabling a constant view of the sun. Atop the structure is a heliostat, which directs sunlight down the angled shaft to a 6½-foot (2 m) lens.

Supporters of the design said that if aluminium was good enough for cadets to fly, fight and die in, then it was good enough for their place of worship. Aluminium is also used for details, from strips atop the wood pews, akin to the leading edge of aircraft wings, to the giant cross that measures 46 by 12 feet (14 x 3.5 m).

U.S. AIR FORCE ACADEMY CHAPEL

WALTER NETSCH

1963

Walter Netsch (1920–2008) was thought by many to have been among the more controversial and independently minded designers working at Skidmore, Owings & Merrill (SOM) in the 1960s and 1970s, the era in which steel-and-glass rectangular boxes held sway across corporate America. Netsch's training at the Massachusetts Institute of Technology and immediate post-World War II work with a small modern suburban architectural firm in Chicago helped to support his individualist edge, compared with the various disciples of Ludwig Mies van der Rohe trained at the Illinois Institute of Technology. This background informs Netsch's U.S. Air Force Academy Chapel near Colorado Springs. When originally planned in 1955, the chapel was set to be a rectilinear building with a folded plate concrete roof. After numerous objections to this scheme, Netsch devised a distinctive, steep, A-framed design of seventeen steel tetrahedron spires, which created an interior space that is approximately 100 feet (30 m) high. Critics referred to it as 'air age Gothic'. The interfaith chapel comprises two levels: the uppermost level is used for Protestant services, whereas the lower one hosts Catholic and Jewish ones. Netsch's bold design makes the chapel a landmark among the mostly horizontal, rectilinear modernist buildings at the academy.

The aluminium-clad steel tetrahedron spires—likened to prefabricated hangars—and stained glass windows within this dynamic hall create a modern equivalent of the well-known 13th-century Gothic royal chapel Sainte-Chapelle in Paris.

Netsch recounted that a senator critiqued the initial box-like concept saying, 'I don't hear the rustle of angels' wings when I look at that building.' Netsch radically revised the plans to the current design, which became a symbol of the Air Force Academy and a National Historic Landmark. Angular, polygonal design forms here paved the way for Netsch's 'field theory'. In this, rotational geometry creates walls and spaces that at first seem arbitrary. He used this system to plan the student centre at Grinnell College (1965) in Iowa and the Miami University Art Museum (1979) in Oxford, Ohio.

Chapel at Illinois Institute of Technology, 1952, Ludwig Mies van der Rohe
Chicago, IL, USA

North Christian Church, 1964, Eero Saarinen
Columbus, IN, USA

This complex reflects both the designer's and the client's interest in modernist design, horses and landscape, as well as in art. The buildings themselves are a sculptural experience akin to walking through a Giorgio de Chirico cityscape painting, with its carefully staged views and pastel wall planes. Barragán's coloured wall planes were intended to create 'an emotional architecture', in which an ideal space would have 'elements of magic, serenity, sorcery and mystery'.

Barragán sought to humanize the severe lines of European modernism through the use of boldly coloured stuccoed walls and the manipulation of light. He created few buildings, perhaps, it has been said, because he thought about each one for weeks, if not months, before creating initial sketches.

FUENTE DE LOS AMANTES

LUIS BARRAGÁN

1966

Born in Mexico, Luis Barragán (1902–1988) trained as an engineer and architect, then travelled throughout Europe, where he was influenced by the works of artist and writer Ferdinand Bac and architect Le Corbusier. Barragán returned to Mexico in 1935 and built several gardens and other works, combining simple, geometric, rectangular forms and walls with bright colours and shafts of light that penetrate spaces at carefully planned intervals. One of the earliest of these is the Chapel and Convent of the Capuchinas Sacramentarias in Tlalpan, begun in 1953. Slightly later works are abstract yet highly coloured sculptures such as Satélite Towers (1957) in Mexico City. His masterpiece of landscape architecture is Fuente de los Amantes (Lovers' Fountain), also in Mexico City. This dramatic composition of coloured wall planes is situated within an open space that is part of a larger complex—house, stables and horse farm—called Cuadra San Cristóbal. Built for Folke Egerström at Los Clubes, it has remained in the family since it was completed. The realities of ongoing maintenance and adjacent land development have pressured the family to put up the complex for sale, and its future remains uncertain.

Fountain and Plaza at Pershing Square,
1994,
Ricardo Legorreta
Los Angeles,
CA, USA

Although not a prolific architect himself, Barragán influenced a number of major international designers such as Louis Kahn, Ricardo Legorreta and Alvaro Siza. Barragán's impact was recognized by an exhibition at the Museum of Modern Art (1977) and he was awarded the Pritzker Architecture Prize in 1980.

After the assassination of President John F. Kennedy in Dallas in 1963, the city was referred to as the 'city of hate'. In order to counter the negative image, Dallas mayor Erik Jonsson instituted a series of goals for the future, one of which focused on design for the city, including a new city hall and municipal centre.

DALLAS CITY HALL
I. M. PEI
1978

Born in China, Ieoh Ming Pei (1917–) is an award-winning architect who is perhaps best known for his beautifully detailed institutional and corporate buildings, often based on a singular, strong geometric form. In addition to Dallas City Hall, these structures include high-profile museums, ranging from the National Gallery of Art's East Building (1978) in Washington, D.C., to the Louvre Pyramid (1989) in Paris. Pei studied architecture in the United States during the 1930s, and graduated from Massachusetts Institute of Technology (MIT) in 1940. He became familiar with the works of Le Corbusier, whom he met when the latter lectured at MIT in 1935. After World War II Pei found initial architectural support from New York powerhouse developer William Zeckendorf and eventually started his own firm in 1955. The first works that projected his bold geometric design preferences were Luce Memorial Chapel (1963) at Tunghai University, Taiwan; a pentagonal air traffic control tower (1965) installed at various airports throughout the United States; and Mesa Laboratory (1967) near Boulder, Colorado. These set the stage for the bold urban design of Dallas City Hall.

The poured concrete, seven-storey structure—560 feet (170 m) long—contains about 691,000 square feet (64,196 sq m), with a 250-seat city council chamber and a 1,325-car garage situated on a plaza of almost 5 acres (2 ha). The building slopes at a 34-degree angle, every floor approximately 9 feet 6 inches (2.9 m) wider than the one below it. Overhanging upper floors serve as sunscreens.

 John F. Kennedy Presidential Library and Museum, 1979, I. M. Pei
Boston, MA, USA

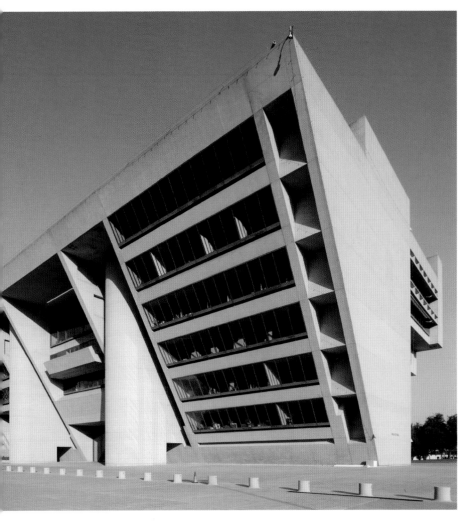

" [Dallas City Hall has] got more strength than finesse.

When Pei was selected as the architect of Dallas City Hall, some feared that his design might be too avant-garde. Yet he convinced them that it was both democratic and rational. Its inverted triangular elevation provides greater office space for 1,400 workstations as the building height increases. The design experiment paved the way for Pei's continued use of overt geometry in his work.

The concrete building with inlaid white marble has a central octagon that is 155 feet (47 m) high. Eight blocks surround this parliamentary chamber, each of which is 110 feet (33 m) high. The connections blend the spaces together, highlighted by dramatic lighting that typifies Kahn's buildings. The central parliament holds 354 members, and there are galleries for visitors, too. Although the chamber is artificially lit from above, this does not interfere with Kahn's natural lighting scheme around the perimeter. The assembly sits adjacent to a lake on 200 acres (81 ha) of gardens, with residences for parliament members.

**NATIONAL ASSEMBLY
LOUIS KAHN
1982**

Louis Kahn (1901–1974) was one of the United States' great architects. His monumental buildings created with simple, bold geometric forms were often informed by philosophical statements, such as 'What does the building want to be?' and 'A room is not a room without natural light'. Born in Estonia, he trained in Philadelphia under Beaux Arts classical modernist Paul Philippe Cret, but was equally influenced by visiting ancient ruins in Italy, Greece and especially Egypt in the early 1950s. Of all his work, the massive National Assembly Building (Jatiyo Sangshad Bhaban) in Sher-e-Bangla Nagar, Bangladesh, is probably the most important. The assembly building is striking for its deeply recessed openings in various geometric shapes articulated by light. Kahn began the design in 1961 and it was completed some twenty years later at a cost of approximately $32 million, almost twice the initial estimate. The architect never saw the completion of his masterpiece, because he died of a heart attack in a public lavatory within New York Penn Station while waiting for a train. His family were not notified for two days because police had an incorrect telephone number.

👁

Salk Institute, 1965,
Louis Kahn
La Jolla, CA, USA

First Unitarian Church, 1969,
Louis Kahn
Rochester, NY, USA

Kimbell Art Museum, 1972,
Louis Kahn
Fort Worth, TX, USA

◎

Kahn developed a theory that differentiated served and servant spaces. Servant spaces were circulatory ones, such as corridors, stairwells and lift cores, whereas served spaces were the primary ones, such as sanctuaries, laboratories, offices and meeting rooms. He would try to separate the two types logically in terms of natural light articulation, size and architectural features. These principles were an outgrowth of his formal Beaux Arts training.

Kahn was invited to work in Bangladesh by Muzharul Islam, the great pioneer of Bengali modernism, and this building was the epitome of his career. It became even more important when Bangladesh declared independence from Pakistan in 1971, making it a symbol of the new democracy. It compares favourably with India's new government buildings of the 1950s by Le Corbusier and other like-styled concrete government buildings that appeared around the world during the 1960s and 1970s.

If people want to see Beaux Arts, it's fine with me. I'm as interested in good architecture as anybody else.

? With their forms balanced on their points, the Cube Houses boldly project the image that architecture can be quirky and does not have to be soberly serious. Rotterdam city official Hans Mentnick, who commissioned Blom, wanted a distinctively designed, high-profile urban renewal project for the city's old harbour site: something that went well beyond predictable modernist buildings.

CUBE HOUSES
PIET BLOM
1984

Piet Blom (1931–1999) was a Dutch architect who trained under Aldo van Eyck. He was known for challenging the status quo with his individualistic interpretations, and his architectural work bears some comparison with painter Piet Mondrian's *Broadway Boogie Woogie* (1942–1943) and the earlier Dutch De Stijl designs of the interwar years. Blom employed a lively palette and also turned geometry upside down in some of his work, in an effort to find a human side to postwar modernism. Housing projects such as the Kasbah (1966) and the Cube Houses in Helmond (1974–1977) and Rotterdam (1977–1984) in particular capture his intention to 'create a society' or a distinctive community. Unfortunately, in 2011, eighteen homes within the Helmond complex were damaged by a fire in the adjacent Theatre 't Speelhuis, which Blom had also designed. The Rotterdam complex was built as a major urban renewal project for the old harbour, which was damaged heavily in World War II. All told, Blom created 270 housing units there along with commercial spaces and parking for 300 cars. However, the buildings continue to adapt to changing times. The complex was renovated in 1988, and in 2009 the larger cubes were replanned into a hostel by Dutch firm Personal Architecture.

Most of the Cube Houses in Rotterdam have three levels: immediately off the street are the kitchen and the living room, the second level, or 'heavenly house', contains the bedrooms, and atop the structure is the light-filled 'leaf hut', or atrium. The core of the building is a vertical hexagon but the other levels all have angular walls at the perimeters. They are constructed mostly of cement and fibreboard covered wood framing.

For each moment of the day and every state of mind there is a different floor to ease one's mind.

The Cube Houses appear elevated like tree houses, hence the pun-like description of them as the 'Blaak Forest', being on Overblaak Street near Blaak metro station. Blom designed the complex 'so that you cannot tell it has been designed by one architect'. It includes a tower that looks like the tip of a pencil and a bridge with shops inspired by the Ponte Vecchio in Florence.

Chicago River Town Houses,
1988,
Harry Weese
Chicago, IL, USA

Moai Pension, 2012,
Studio Koosino
Gyeonggi-do, near Seoul,
South Korea

After a car accident in 1971 made Rossi think about his mortality, he began to conceive his theoretical city of the dead. This cemetery is the result of that life-changing event. The severe elevation of the cube-like red stucco 'monument' sits within a larger series of low buildings, all projecting a sombre image appropriate to their function. Completely devoid of ornamentation, the main sanctuary features symmetrical rows of raw box-like windows, almost a high-rise monument within this cemetery city. Indeed, the grid facade is Rossi's masterpiece, and it may well have had an impact on other architects working in the 1970s and 1980s whose elevations are equally severe.

Central Economics and Mathematics Institute, 1978, Leonid Pavlov
Moscow, Russia

Institut du Monde Arabe, 1988, Jean Nouvel
Paris, France

The sober interior intended for human remains is partly reflected on the outside. The windows illuminate the interior rows with a red glow from the like-coloured exterior stucco. Inside, raw concrete boxes form grids that are cruciform in shape.

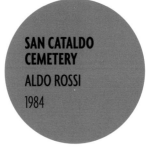

SAN CATALDO CEMETERY

ALDO ROSSI

1984

Aldo Rossi (1931–1997) was an internationally recognized Italian architect and designer who graduated from the Polytechnic University of Milan in 1959. Some of his best-known works range from tableware and home furnishings for Alessi to the Teatro del Mondo installation at the Venice Biennale (1979), a floating theatre that drew upon the traditions of similar Venetian structures. Rossi's philosophy was that urban environments grow and change over time in layers of history provided by tangible landmarks. He published these views in *The Architecture of the City* (*L'architettura della città*) in 1966. Perhaps the architect's best-known project in relation to these ideas is the 'city of the dead', which found tangible expression in the enigmatic Cemetery of San Cataldo in Modena. Although he won the commission in a competition in collaboration with Gianni Braghieri in 1971, and construction began in 1978, the project remains largely incomplete.

"

[Teatro del Mondo is] a place where architecture ended and the world of the imagination began.

Rossi's severe grid-like buildings were influenced by the paintings of Giorgio de Chirico, such as *The Enigma of a Day* (1914), and the so-called Rationalist buildings of Giuseppe Terragni, particularly the fascist headquarters Casa del Fascio (1936) in Como, Italy.

MOCA director Richard Koshalek was instrumental in working with the trustees in the selection of Isozaki and navigating the politics to bring the building to a successful conclusion, complete with Isozaki's trademark barrel vault and undulating wall atop the plaza. The inclusion of these elements alongside other geometric forms set the architect apart. The publicity associated with this building did not lead to other museums in the United States for Isozaki, but rather to corporate work for Disney.

Gunma Museum of Fine Arts, 1974, Arata Isozaki Takasaki, Japan

Palau D'Esports Sant Jordi, 1990, Arata Isozaki Barcelona, Spain

MUSEUM OF CONTEMPORARY ART
ARATA ISOZAKI
1986

Arata Isozaki (1931–) studied at the University of Tokyo under Kenzo Tange, graduating in 1954. He started his current firm in 1963, and since then has been one of several Japanese architects who have achieved widespread popularity and awards for architectural and product designs across the globe. Isozaki broke into the U.S. market with his first U.S. building: the Museum of Contemporary Art (MOCA) in Los Angeles. The building's commission, awarded in 1981, was said to have been revised substantially—thirty-six times—by a somewhat contentious board before being set in stone. Now known as the main branch of MOCA, it was an important project of its kind because it was funded by a percent for art programme as part of the California Plaza redevelopment in the Bunker Hill neighbourhood. The building is designed around a terraced courtyard, and the museum's main exhibition spaces are housed under the courtyard, illuminated by pyramidal skylights. Geometrically, the composition conforms to the principles of the golden section seen in much Western art, but overall the structure is characterized by Isozaki's characteristic barrel vault. Today the building houses MOCA's permanent collection.

Isozaki's first U.S. works were installations in New York's Cooper Hewitt Design Museum (1976 and 1979), and in Chicago's Merchandise Mart during Neocon (1982). Public recognition of these exhibits paved the way for MOCA.

Isozaki's Indian red sandstone building with Canadian red granite details replaced the so-called Temporary Contemporary (1983) loft renovation designed by Frank Gehry (known today as MOCA's Geffen Building). Isozaki's postmodern arched design was, like many of his buildings at the time, an homage to the arched massing in Neoclassical works by Claude Nicolas Ledoux and to Le Corbusier's bold forms.

This is one of seven major Bahá'í temples across the world. Each is distinct yet shares some basic concepts, particularly in its polygonal, nine-sided, usually domed form. Many think that the mandala is the oldest of Indian sacred forms but the lotus flower is a sacred flower to Indians, Hindus and Buddhists alike.

LOTUS TEMPLE
FARIBORZ SAHBA
1986

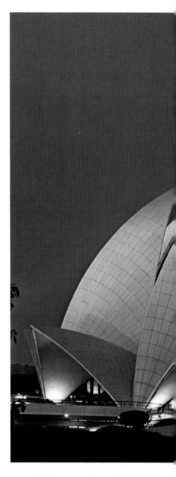

Iranian-born Canadian architect Fariborz Sahba (1948–) earned his master's degree in architecture from the University of Tehran in 1972, having been encouraged as a youth by his mother to pursue the profession. After graduation he participated with others in designing buildings in Iran, but at the age of twenty-eight the architect earned the job opportunity of a lifetime and was selected to design the Bahá'í House of Worship, also known as the Lotus Temple, in Bahapur, New Delhi, India. The Bahá'í faith was founded in 1863 in what is now Iran by Bahá'u'lláh, and followers believe in the oneness of God, of religion and of humankind. They also believe in Bahá'u'lláh as a prophet or God's messenger, equal to Moses, Jesus or Buddha, for example. The religion began with some seventy worshippers but it has grown today to have a following of more than 5 million, with major temples in Australia, Germany, India, Kampala, Uganda, the United States and Western Samoa. The glistening white concrete structure in New Delhi has surpassed its function as a place of worship to become an architectural icon of the city. Because of the high number of visitors to the site (more than 4.5 million people per year), the project also includes a visitor centre with a 500-seat auditorium, exhibition galleries and offices, completed in 2002.

The concrete building is clad in white Grecian marble and sits in 26 acres (10.5 ha). The structure consists of twenty-seven marble-clad 'petals' or columns organized in groups of three to create nine sides. The central space is more than 131 feet (40 m) high.

Having won the competition to design the Lotus Temple in 1976, Sahba visited more than a hundred temples in India before choosing the lotus flower as an important sacred image and a distinctive architectural symbol. With modern air conditioning deemed too costly, he designed 'natural ventilation', based on the principle of desert wind towers, with openings in the building's basement and the dome's top. Because of the temple's success, the architect received commissions for other major Bahá'í sites, such as the terraced gardens of the Shrine of the Báb (2001) in Haifa, Israel.

Cathedral of Brasília, 1970, Oscar Niemeyer
Brasília, Brazil

Sydney Opera House, 1973, Jørn Utzon
Sydney, Australia

Ando's style of building is intended, like that of many modernists, to 'reform society'. His love of building surfaces, details and materials expressed in simple concrete walls and his love of light clearly define this little church. He uses these techniques in many of his buildings, but perhaps this tiny church's budget restraints helped to make it the major monument that it now is.

CHURCH OF THE LIGHT

TADAO ANDO

1989

Osaka-born Tadao Ando (1941–) is a professional boxer and self-taught architect. His spiritual works fuelled his rapid rise to recognition as one of the world's most celebrated architects.

Ando's strongest designs combine the beauty of natural light and natural contexts, such as water, with the strength and almost silky fabric-like texture of poured concrete walls to produce a serene environment. His amazingly consistent performance in creating striking yet simple Zen-like experiences within buildings has garnered him numerous international awards. One such building is the Church of the Light in the Ibaraki section of Osaka. This tiny church of roughly 1,200 square feet (113 sq m) projects a powerful though quiet beauty, especially when morning light shines through the cross-like fenestration at the eastern end of the sanctuary. Ando's small-scale buildings, which include chapels, galleries and private houses, are gem-like in their understated, tranquil, yet powerful aesthetics. However, the architect has also fulfilled major commissions in the 21st century that project a similar image, ranging from the Pulitzer Foundation for the Arts (2001) in St. Louis, Missouri, to the Modern Art Museum (2002) in Fort Worth, Texas, and the Langen Foundation (2004) in Hombroich, Neuss, Germany.

In all my works, light is an important controlling factor.

Church on the Water, 1988, Tadao Ando
Tomamu, Hokkaido, Japan

Japanese Screen Gallery, 1992, Tadao Ando
Art Institute of Chicago, IL, USA

Characteristic of many of Ando's works, the church's reinforced concrete walls have an almost perfectly smooth fabric-like texture. The space was, for a time, intended to be unroofed because the congregation could not afford a roof, but the contractor agreed to donate it. Recycled wooden scaffolding was used for the benches and floorboards. The simple, serene, almost empty volume, dramatically lit, characterizes some of Ando's other works, too, particularly ones that are chapel-like in scale.

Ando decided to become an architect after visiting shrines and temples in Nara and Kyoto, and then extending his visits to Tokyo to see Frank Lloyd Wright's Imperial Hotel (1923; demolished 1968). He read books by Le Corbusier and visited the architect's Unité d'Habitation (1952) in Marseille, France, admiring its poured concrete structure.

This simple yet powerful design was selected by President Mitterrand because of its 'purity and strength'. Von Spreckelsen was no stranger to cubes in his church designs, as witnessed in the Vangede Church (1974) at Gentofte and the Stavnsholt Church (1981) at Farum, both in Denmark. He enlarged the principle here to gigantic size with the assistance of Danish engineer and educational colleague Erik Reitzel. Although the cubic form is rare at this scale, large cubic buildings have seen a rebirth in the past few years.

Cube Tube, 2010,
SAKO Architects
Jinhua, Zhejiang
Province, China

*Emerson
College*, 2014,
Thom Mayne
Los Angeles,
CA, USA

LA GRANDE ARCHE DE LA DÉFENSE
JOHANN OTTO VON SPRECKELSEN
1989

A suburb west of Paris, La Défense is a business community and cultural tourism destination that sees more than 2 million visitors a year because of monuments such as La Grande Arche de la Défense by Danish architect Johann Otto von Spreckelsen (1929–1987), public sculptures by artists such as Alexander Calder, Joan Miró and Richard Serra, and a host of skyscrapers by A-list architects. During the 1980s, at the same time as this mega office park was being developed, French president François Mitterrand oversaw the Grands Projets architectural programme across Paris. The most important of these projects was a competition in 1982 to design a bicentennial monument to the French Revolution (1789), and it was won, surprisingly, by von Spreckelsen, an architectural educator with only a few modernist masonry churches to his credit. Construction began in 1985 but von Spreckelsen resigned from the team the following year. Paul Andreu of Aéroports de Paris, known for airport commissions across the globe, was the design associate and he led the project to completion. The monument sits on a 6-mile (10-km) axis to Paris's city centre, providing a visual counterpoint to the historic Arc de Triomphe (1836).

The steel-and-concrete arch clad with Carrara marble is almost cubical and measures approximately 360 feet (110 m) on each side. It is shifted slightly from its axis by a little more than 6 degrees, so that its foundations could be accommodated around the railway stations underneath, and weighs 300,000 tons or thirty times the weight of the Eiffel Tower. La Grande Arche de la Défense houses offices in its sides. Originally it also had an observation deck and gourmet restaurant at the top, but a lift accident in 2010 caused their permanent closure. Von Spreckelsen's contemporary church designs in Denmark were cubical, too, so this structure is a clear extension of his preferences.

Following the success of the Centre Georges Pompidou (1977) by Richard Rogers and Renzo Piano, the Grands Projets were directed by two French presidents: Valéry Giscard d'Estaing and François Mitterrand. Mitterrand stated: 'Beauty stimulates curiosity. . . . My wish is that the major projects help us to understand our roots and our history, that they will permit us to foresee the future and to conquer it.'

We were under heavy constraints in constructing a 'modern Arc de Triomphe' that continued the historic east–west axis in Paris.
PAUL ANDREU

The government-funded Grands Projets created cultural buildings in Paris to commemorate the bicentenary of the French Revolution. They include Nouvel's Institut du Monde Arabe; Musée d'Orsay (1986) by Gae Aulenti; Parc de la Villette (1987) by Bernard Tschumi; and Louvre Pyramid (1989) by I.M. Pei.

FONDATION CARTIER
JEAN NOUVEL
1994

Jean Nouvel (1945–) is a high-profile French architect who studied at the Ecole des Beaux-Arts in Paris and was apprenticed to architects Claude Parent and Paul Virilio. Active within architecturally intellectual circles in Paris, Nouvel was part of the team that organized the competition for Les Halles de Paris (1977). However, his big break came in 1981 when he won the competition to design the Institut du Monde Arabe. Completed in 1987, this simple glass-and-steel building incorporates photoelectric cells that control a lace-like metallic screen, which modulates the light entering the building, thus providing sunscreening in the tradition of Islamic architecture. The building catapulted Nouvel to international recognition and numerous awards, as well as launching him on a career that led to buildings across Europe, and in Korea and Qatar, too. Fondation Cartier in Paris is perhaps the most elegantly beautiful of these. Although not officially one of the government-sponsored Grands Projets, this private nonprofit building raised the bar for Parisian architecture, and provides an excellent contemporary art exhibition venue. The jewel box-like building is situated in a wooded wildflower garden designed by German artist Lothar Baumgarten. Titled 'Theatrum Botanicum', the greenery penetrates the lobby and the entrance facade.

Nouvel's steel-and-glass building is 102 feet (31 m) high. It includes offices, exhibition galleries and underground parking facilities. Movable glass walls are 26 feet (8 m) high—the height of the main exhibition space—and open directly onto the garden.

The transparency and rigorous detailing of Fondation Cartier are continuations of qualities seen in the Institut du Monde Arabe, and can be found consistently in other work by Nouvel, who referred to the building's transparency as an 'interplay between structure and nature'. Confirmation of this is found in the skeletal walls that reveal landscape beyond and office personnel within. This interplay between a minimalist grid and nature prefigures similar interactions in later Nouvel projects, such as One Central Park (2014) in Sydney, Australia.

Within the garden is an historic cedar 'Tree of Liberty' that poet François-René de Chateaubriand planted in 1823.

Reina Sofía Art Centre Expansion, 2005, Jean Nouvel
Madrid, Spain

This strong visual statement creates a landmark that screams 'art school' within the neighbourhood. The $42.5 million expansion of OCAD was part of the city's SuperBuild programme (2000) to support post-secondary educational institutions. The entire project commemorated the school's 125th anniversary. It not only included the expansion spaces that Alsop designed, but also renovation of the existing building below.

SHARP CENTRE FOR DESIGN
WILL ALSOP
2004

English architect Will Alsop (1947–) has created a number of distinctive, sometimes controversial, buildings. The award-winning Sharp Centre for Design at the Ontario College of Art and Design (OCAD) is no exception.

Alsop left school to be an architect's apprentice and initially was most influenced by Henry Bird of the Northampton School of Art. He later studied at the Architectural Association in London. In 2004 he published a book titled *Supercity*, which proposed a futuristic metropolis connecting Liverpool and Hull in England on the M62 motorway, an idea that elicited much discussion and demonstrated Alsop's interest in the big picture. After working in a variety of firms and teaching sculpture, he established his current practice, aLL Design, in 2011. The Sharp Centre for Design was constructed at a venerable art school with roots that can be traced back to 1876 and campus buildings that are a hodge-podge of various designs. In contrast to Alsop's slightly earlier buildings that mostly created bold overall forms, but were more traditionally detailed in terms of a modernist vocabulary, this playful slab—sometimes described as a tabletop—is perched atop colourful pencil-like towers. The composition projects the Pop image of an eraser spiked with pencils.

Alsop's architectural influences include Sir John Soane, Le Corbusier and Ludwig Mies van der Rohe: Soane's quirky boldness of form, Le Corbusier's sense of grand scale and some of the precision of Mies. Art teacher Henry Bird had Alsop draw and redraw a brick's perfect lines, similar to the way in which Mies's students detailed bricks that round the corner.

Alsop likens his work to abstract painting because he likes the opportunity to change the work during the process and to give chance an impact on architectural design as much as planning. He designed the interiors so that spaces could be adapted to future student needs. The interiors were not '. . . too precious . . . students should be able to throw a bucket of paint without destroying the design'.

I am slightly jealous of the Seattle Library by Rem Koolhaas. I haven't seen it in the flesh but from photographs in publications, it is a magnificent building.

Cardiff Bay Visitor Centre, 1991, Will Alsop
Cardiff, Wales

Ferry Terminal, 1993, Will Alsop
Hamburg, Germany

Peckham Library, 2000, Will Alsop
London, UK

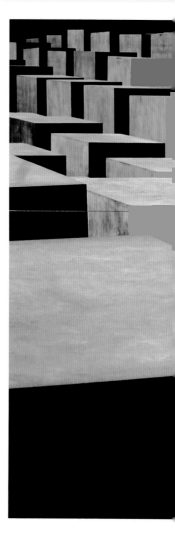

The memorial consists of 2,711 concrete slabs of varying heights, positioned grid-like upon an undulating field of some 4.7 acres (1.9 ha) near the Brandenburg Gate. Each block is 7 feet 10 inches (2.4 m) long and 3 feet 1 inch (0.95 m) wide.

HOLOCAUST MEMORIAL

PETER EISENMAN

2004

New Jersey-born Peter Eisenman (1932–) is arguably the most intellectually theoretical of U.S. architects. He has earned degrees from Cornell, Columbia and the University of Cambridge, and his architectural works were forerunners of what became known as Deconstructivism. Eisenman's designs are typified by fragmented modernist forms that relate to historic and archaeological grids—actual and perceived—within and adjacent to a building site. A notable example is the Wexner Center for the Arts (1989) at Ohio State University, where the layers of exterior lattice, interior structure and fragmented brick turrets recall the campus grid at different times and the form of a demolished armoury. These elements are also evident in the anonymous concrete blocks within Berlin's Holocaust Memorial, dedicated on 10 May 2005, for the sixtieth anniversary of VE (Victory in Europe) Day.

The commission was awarded to Eisenman and sculptor Richard Serra in 1997, but Serra withdrew the following year. Chancellor of Germany Helmut Kohl and the Bundestag approved Eisenman's final design on 25 June 1999, with the addition of a museum-like information centre.

There is no goal, no end, no working one's way in or out.

IBA Social Housing at Checkpoint Charlie, 1985, Peter Eisenman Berlin, Germany

Eisenman intended to project a sense of uneasiness, uncertainty and confusion within the layout: some slabs are more than 15 feet (4.5 m) high making it difficult for visitors to get their bearings. Although the grid connotes order, when order goes beyond human scale it becomes inhumane and overwhelming. As in the case of the architect's other projects, the grid here relates to the street system of Berlin.

The ICA was constructed in association with Perry Dean Rogers. Its striking facade is made of equally scaled alternating vertical panels of transparent and translucent glass, with glass and metal providing a tight planar skin around the perimeter of the structure. The building contains approximately 65,000 square feet (6,038 sq m), of which 18,000 square feet (1,672 sq m) is devoted to museum galleries, with movable walls and polished concrete floors. A media centre is hung below. The glazed walls within the 330-seat theatre can be adjusted from transparent to opaque, depending upon performance needs within.

Peckham Library, 2000, Will Alsop London, UK

Seattle Public Library, 2004, Rem Koolhaas Seattle, WA, USA

The ICA is said to have used enough steel to manufacture 350 SUVs, and the lift can hold seventy-two people.

INSTITUTE OF CONTEMPORARY ART DILLER, SCOFIDIO AND RENFRO 2006

Elizabeth Diller (1954–) and Ricardo Scofidio (1935–) began their New York firm in 1979 and were joined in 1997 by Charles Renfro (1964–), who became a partner in 2004. Husband and wife Scofidio and Diller were the first architects to be awarded a MacArthur Fellowship, or 'Genius Grant', in 1999. Their early projects were akin to conceptual art exhibitions and performance art, and they arrived on the scene internationally with the Blur Building at Expo 2002 in Yverdon, Switzerland. Based on the tensile structures of U.S. engineer and architect Richard Buckminster Fuller, this media pavilion on the banks of Lake Neuchâtel featured an interactive experience of lake water sprayed in a mist through thousands of nozzles, creating an artificial, domical cloud some 300 feet (91 m) wide by 200 feet (61 m) deep and 65 feet (20 m) high. This was a very creative, large piece of performance architecture, the exposure of which helped secure subsequent projects such as the Institute of Contemporary Art (ICA) in Boston, a \$51-million commission that they won in competition. It was the first museum to be built in the city in one hundred years.

The somewhat untested Diller, Scofidio and Renfro won the ICA commission perhaps because of their attitudes towards contemporary art as much as their architectural experience. Certainly the Blur Building pavilion in 2002 had to have made some impact on anyone interested in contemporary art. Furthermore, their architectural design, which one critic called 'top heavy', recalls other institutional buildings with similar massing designed by Rem Koolhaas, Will Alsop and Zaha Hadid, among others.

The Fan Pier location of the ICA engages the waterfront visually and physically, as expressed in the box-like cantilevered gallery spaces, which overlook Boston's inner harbour, and a glass lift that offers waterfront views. The wooden Harbor Walk is referenced by the theatre floor and ceiling, and the sliding glass doors of the café expand the facility's openness towards the harbour. Despite these positive site references, critics complain that the building turns its back on the land.

Naïveté gets us a long way. We relentlessly pursue getting this done even if the idea seems totally nuts, like building a cloud.

ELIZABETH DILLER

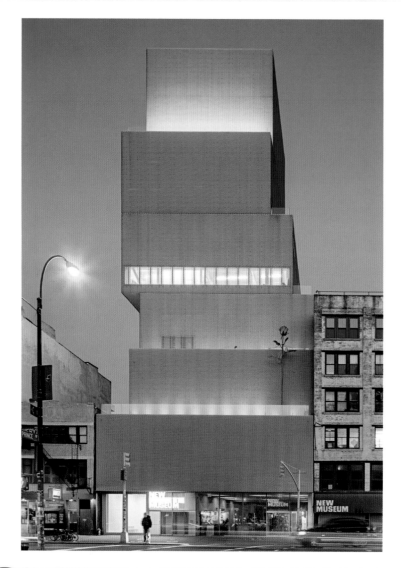

SANAA's work before the New Museum had been consistently modernist, favouring minimal steel structures and large planes of glass. This vertically stacked, blocky design came out of the museum's restrictive site and the architects' goal to create a building that felt both 'elegant and urban'. The latter relates to the variety of scale and massing that can be seen in the neighbourhood's existing fabric.

NEW MUSEUM OF CONTEMPORARY ART

SANAA

2007

Japanese architects Kazuyo Sejima (1956–) and Ryue Nishizawa (1966–) created the Tokyo-based firm SANAA in 1995, and together they have designed some architecturally innovative museum structures. The New Museum of Contemporary Art in New York City is probably their most creative, and in a sense it allowed them to break out of the box in comparison to their other work. Together Sejima and Nishizawa have designed architectural gems such as the minimally modernist Glass Pavilion for the Toledo Museum of Art (2006) in Ohio. This was SANAA's first building in the United States, and the beautifully detailed galleries doubtless had some impact on the firm being selected to design the New Museum of Contemporary Art and also influenced its successful competition entry in 2006 for Louvre Lens (2012) in France. Furthermore, SANAA's simple yet striking designs helped garner the prestigious Pritzker Architecture Prize in 2010. The New Museum building was essentially this institution's first permanent headquarters devoted to contemporary art. The $50 million project was built in collaboration with U.S. associate architects, Gensler, and when the building opened in 2007 *Condé Nast Traveller* named it one of the new seven wonders of the architectural world.

This seven-storey steel building clad in anodized aluminium mesh contains 58,700 square feet (5,453 sq m) piled up like irregularly stacked boxes. The shifted shapes and aluminium skin animate the building's mass, making it changeable with the vagaries of weather and sunlight. SANAA felt that this reflects comparable qualities in contemporary art. Typically, the interiors are monochromatically white, with polished grey concrete floors, except for green lift cars and red super-graphic cherry blossom walls in the lavatories.

Glass Pavilion, Toledo Museum of Art, 2006,
SANAA
Toledo, OH, USA

Louvre Lens, 2012, SANAA
Lens, France

The architects wanted to respond to the history and mission of the art institution as well as the scruffy Bowery neighbourhood, known historically for housing society's outsiders. SANAA stated that both the Bowery and the New Museum were 'accepting, open and embracing every idiosyncrasy in an unprejudiced manner'.

There is a generic quality to white that we like.
KAZUYO SEJIMA

Because of his architectural reputation in disaster relief, Ban was invited by church officials to go to New Zealand after the earthquake. His facility with paper temporary constructions also earned him the Pritzker Architecture Prize in 2014 not only for his excellent, creative design solutions with recyclable materials, but also because he has made 'a significant and consistent contribution to humanity'.

CARDBOARD CATHEDRAL
SHIGERU BAN
2013

Tokyo-born and trained Shigeru Ban (1957–) dreamed of being a carpenter and then an architect because of his love of drawing and structural modelling using bamboo and paper. In architectural books he encountered the work of John Hejduk and was inspired to study under him at Cooper Union for the Advancement of Science and Art in 1980. Ban returned to Tokyo in 1985 and opened his own architectural office. He first began to experiment with paper tube constructions in his Alvar Aalto exhibition installation (1986). He created paper log houses after the Kobe earthquake in 1995 and paper emergency shelters for the United Nations in 1999 to help alleviate housing conditions for the millions of refugees from the civil war in Rwanda. Later variants include temporary housing after natural disasters in Turkey (2000), India (2001), Haiti (2010), Japan (2011) and China (2014). Ban's cardboard-tubed cathedral in Christchurch, New Zealand, is a tangible, very creative symbol of reconstruction after the great earthquake in 2011. Beyond his facility with recyclable temporary buildings, Ban conscientiously practises a sustainable architecture even in his more permanent structures, such as the Tamedia Building (2013) in Zurich, built using interlocked timbers without metal hardware or adhesive.

Working in collaboration with architects Warren and Mahoney, Ban created an A-frame of ninety-six cardboard tubes some 78 feet (24 m) high. Each tube weighs approximately 1,000 pounds (454 kg) and they sit atop 20-foot-long (6-m) shipping containers. Local suppliers could not make truly structural tubes, so they are reinforced with wood beams and coated with flame retardants and waterproof polyurethane. The polycarbonate roof illuminates the space below as do the stained glass windows at one end.

Onagawa Community Centre, 2011, Shigeru Ban
Miyagi, Japan

Paper Nursery School, 2014, Shigeru Ban
Ya'an City, Sichuan, China

Ban's brief was to design a temporary cathedral that could seat 700. Although it was intended as a transitional structure, legal problems related to insurance payouts, fund-raising timing for the new structure and the need for a sturdy building that could last a long time all complicated the situation and the budget, which reached almost NZ $6 million.

Everyone used to want to be star architects. That's no longer the case.

The ten-storey steel-and-concrete structure, clad in aluminium sunscreens, houses 217 students, who study television and film, in the residential towers that form the sides of the cube. The cube's centre contains an anthropomorphically designed glazed structure with studios, offices and classrooms.

EMERSON COLLEGE
THOM MAYNE
2014

Trained at the University of Southern California, Thom Mayne (1944–) is the design force behind Morphosis, a Los Angeles firm that he cofounded in 1972. After earning his master's degree in architecture at Harvard in 1978, he returned to Morphosis and continued his leadership. Mayne's institutional and governmental work is characterized by bold, large-scale, geometric forms. These include buildings at the universities of Toronto (2000) and Cincinnati (2006) as well as Cooper Union (2009) in New York and structures for the United States Federal Government as part of the Design Excellence Program. His building for Emerson College on Sunset Boulevard in Los Angeles creates a strong street presence. Its open cube makes it an unmistakable landmark on the strip, much as La Grande Arche de la Défense (1989) in Paris is the mega landmark of the suburb of La Défense.

Mayne cofounded the Southern California Institute of Architecture in 1972. In this, he and his colleagues intended to bring to Los Angeles the kind of critical thought that existed at the Institute for Architecture and Urban Studies and Cooper Union, both in New York, and the Architectural Association in London.

" *The idea of Boston students coming to L.A., and how interesting it was to make an environment that was very L.A.*

University of Toronto Graduate Housing, 2000, Thom Mayne
Toronto, Canada

Cooper Union, 2009, Thom Mayne
New York, NY, USA

Although the college projects a strong geometry in keeping with all of Mayne's works, he created it as 'a critique of an institutional building as a big block'. On one level the massive cube is a monument on Sunset Boulevard, but on another level, the small aluminium panels within the courtyard and the open informal performance space within the cube itself help to break down the block into 'a little town'.

CHAPTER TWO
SPACE AGE

Space travel was unique to the second half of the 20th century, and the scientific achievements that made it possible also influenced myriad cultural developments, including in the field of architecture. The buildings in this chapter range from monuments to the space age—in Berlin, Brussels, Leicester, Montreal, Moscow and the New Mexico desert—to designs that share the fantasy if not the reality of space age aesthetics. For example, structures by architects Günther Domenig and Future Systems appear to reference science fiction or even alien imagery. Just as the space programme fostered new materials and technology, architects followed suit: Allison Dring created pollution-neutralizing facade tiles, and Zaha Hadid and Frank Gehry created otherworldly designs developed using aerospace-based computer programs.

❬ U.S. Pavilion Expo '67, Montreal, Canada

The Atomium comprises nine large spheres—each with a diameter of 59 feet (18 m)—connected by twenty tubes, and the entire complex is supported by three pillars. Escalators and staircases through the tubes connect to exhibition and restaurant spaces within the spheres. The steel structure was originally clad in aluminium and stands 335 feet (102 m) high. In 2009 the aluminium cladding was replaced by stainless steel, and some of the historic panels were sold to collectors to help finance the restoration.

Unisphere, New York World's Fair, 1964, Gilmore Clarke
Flushing Meadow Park, New York, NY, USA

Taking a cue from the image of airline stewardesses, the organizers of the fair hired 300 multilingual hostesses and dressed them in red blazers and blue caps to assist the 41 million visitors.

ATOMIUM
ANDRÉ WATERKEYN, ANDRÉ POLAK AND JEAN POLAK
1958

The Atomium theme structure built for Expo '58 in the Heizelpark in Brussels follows in the tradition of the New York theme buildings—the Trylon and Perisphere—created for the 1939–1940 New York World's Fair, which were considered to be the first great theme structures of 20th-century world's fairs. These massive geometric forms designed by Wallace Harrison and Jacques André Fouilhoux contained exhibits designed by Henry Dreyfuss. The constructions were built of temporary materials, and they were intended to be demolished after the fair. Fortunately the still extant Atomium was built of more permanent steel. This masterpiece is the work of Belgian engineer André Waterkeyn (1917–2005) with its interiors designed by architects André (1914–1988) and Jean (1920–2012) Polak. The structure projected the image of the peaceful use of nuclear energy. Although it was not intended originally to be a permanent building, the Atomium was so popular that it has now been restored as a tourist attraction. It contains exhibits of the Expo '58 fair and temporary architecture and design exhibits, as well as a children's sphere, an observatory and a restaurant in the uppermost sphere. It hosts 600,000 visitors each year.

Expo '58's celebration of science coincided with the International Geophysical Year (1957–1958), which promoted free exchange of scientific information. It was also when the Soviet Union and the United States began to compete in the space race. At Expo '58 the Soviet pavilion displayed full-size replicas of Sputnik I and II, while the U.S. Pavilion had no space presence, its focus instead being on consumer items.

Waterkeyn was asked to design a structure for the fair that would showcase Belgian engineering prowess. The Atomium represents the cell of an iron crystal enlarged 165 billion times. It also projected a positive peaceful image of nuclear power and science in the postwar era. Because of the success of that image, planners at the Seattle and New York fairs in the 1960s tried to top it with their own theme structures.

? The architectural team was the best design talent in the city at the time. Together they planned the airport in 1958 as one in which a central domed building connected to the terminals surrounding it. Their plan was never realized, but what did result was the space-age curved structure known as the Theme Building, which has been an architectural symbol of this airport since it was built. It is an expressive masterpiece of futuristic design appropriate for the jet age.

The reinforced concrete building—135 feet (41 m) high—has a restaurant hung between its spindly, parabolically arched legs. An observation deck is situated atop. The landmark building underwent a thorough renovation in 2010, complete with stucco resurfacing of the concrete and a mass damper atop to resist earthquake damage.

Success is that old ABC—ability, breaks and courage.
CHARLES LUCKMAN

*Lambert-St. Louis
International Airport*, 1956,
Hellmuth, Yamasaki, Leinweber
St. Louis, MO, USA

*TWA Terminal, Kennedy
International Airport*, 1962,
Eero Saarinen
New York, NY, USA

**THEME BUILDING
PEREIRA AND LUCKMAN
1961**

Jet airliners of the late 1950s and early 1960s made an enormous impact across the globe, not only in the democratization of air travel, but also in the revitalization of airline corporate identity, airliner interiors and airport terminals. Airport authorities had to radically update existing facilities and plan additional ones for the new, sometimes larger, machines. Los Angeles International Airport (LAX) was one of those that witnessed a dramatic transformation. The airport was initially called Mines Field, and its first Mission-style building, which opened in 1929 as the Curtiss-Wright depot and hangar, still sits on the LAX grounds. Its tiny scale gives the sense of the dramatic jet-age expansion that took place here. LAX did not officially become Los Angeles's main airport until the 1940s, and its runways were extended during the early to mid 1950s in anticipation of the jet age. In 1958 a team of Los Angeles's best architects was selected for replanning the terminals, led by the firm Pereira and Luckman, founded by William Pereira (1909–1985) and Charles Luckman (1909–1999). Although their plans for LAX were never fully realized, the distinctive Theme Building, designed by Pereira's assistant, James Langenheim, was built, and its iconic white form has since become a landmark on the LAX site.

William Pereira was also a designer for films, and his work can be seen in *This Gun for Hire (1942)*, *Jane Eyre* (1943), *Johnny Angel* (1945) and *From This Day Forward* (1946), for example.

Both Luckman and Pereira made important design contributions, and when they parted in 1959 each made their individual mark. Luckman is best known for Prudential Tower (1964) in Boston and Madison Square Garden (1968) in New York, whereas Pereira's dramatic buildings include Giesel Library (1970) in San Diego and Transamerica Pyramid (1972) in San Francisco.

? Graham's initial concept was for a saucer-like restaurant and he filed a patent in 1961. He worked with engineer Steinbrueck, who proposed the tower, and local hotel entrepreneur Eddie Carlson. Carlson is said to have combined both tower and restaurant in a napkin sketch, based on his familiarity with the Television Tower (1956) in Stuttgart, Germany. Graham's revolving restaurant influenced dozens of later designs.

**SPACE NEEDLE
JOHN GRAHAM
1962**

John Graham Jr (1908–1991) was the son of architect John Graham and he inherited his father's Seattle firm. After completing his education at Yale, John Jr took over the business in 1946 and specialized in commercial buildings, especially shopping centres. His Northgate Mall (1950) is one of the earliest enclosed shopping centres in the United States. The architect's best-known work, however, is the Space Needle in Seattle, a design that is also claimed by engineering consultant Victor Steinbrueck. The Space Needle concept was in conformance with the overall aerospace theme of the Century 21 Exposition of 1962, also known as the Seattle World's Fair, under the direction of architect Paul Thiry. It was not officially part of the fair but was a private venture built at a cost of $4.5 million on adjacent land, purchased from the city for $75,000. Since its completion, the Space Needle has become an icon of Seattle, more so than other survivors of the fair, such as the Monorail and the Pacific Science Center (originally the Science Pavilion containing the Boeing-sponsored Spacearium). The latter was designed by Seattle-born Minoru Yamasaki, who was later architect for the World Trade Center (1972, destroyed) in New York City.

The steel-and-concrete tower is 605 feet (184 m) high, and there is an observation deck, restaurant and gift shop at the top, at a height of 500 feet (152 m). Originally, the tower's palette was orbital olive, astronaut white, re-entry red and galaxy gold. The complex has been renovated several times, and the current light beam atop was installed to celebrate the millennium in 2000. During the Century 21 Exposition, the Space Needle had more than 2 million visitors.

Northgate Mall, 1950,
John Graham
Seattle, WA, USA

Washington Plaza Hotel, 1969,
John Graham
Seattle, WA, USA

English-born John Graham Sr started his architectural practice in Seattle in 1900. He designed industrial and commercial buildings, and some of the most prominent ones were in Seattle: the Frederick & Nelson Store, now Nordstrom (1918), and the Bon Marché, later Macy's (1928). These commercial jobs laid the groundwork for the firm's post-World War II expansion, particularly with shopping centres.

Elvis Presley starred in the film *It Happened at the World's Fair* (1963), which featured scenes of the fair in Seattle, including Elvis and actress Joan O'Brien dining in the restaurant atop the Space Needle.

The steel structure is 350 feet (107 m) high and clad in titanium. It has been said that the head of the Soviet space programme, Sergei Korolev, suggested using this durable material because it would showcase the nation's technical superiority. Its use also recalls the story that Korolev wanted Sputnik I to be so highly polished that it could be seen easily from Earth. The shaft sits atop a masonry base with traditional bas-reliefs of the early cosmonauts, engineers, scientists, workers and even the dog Laika.

Statue of Yuri Gagarin,
1980, Pavel Bondarenko
Yuri Gagarin Square,
Moscow, Russia

Cosmonaut Monument,
1980, B. V. Edunov
Kaliningrad, Russia

Named after the first human to travel into space, Yuri's Night is celebrated worldwide on 12 April, the anniversary of his orbital flight, with events that draw attention to space flight.

MONUMENT TO THE CONQUERORS OF SPACE
A. P. FAIDYSH-KRANDIEVSKY
1964

4 October 1957 marked a game changer in the Cold War (1948–1989) between the United States and the Soviet Union, when the Russians launched the first artificial satellite, Sputnik I. They repeated this a month later with Sputnik II, which carried the first dog into space. The United States competed with Explorer 1 and Vanguard 1 a year later. However, the Russians outdid the Americans again when cosmonaut Yuri Gagarin became the first human to orbit the Earth on 12 April 1961. The United States could not match this until astronaut John Glenn also orbited the Earth almost a year later, on 20 February 1962. The Russians were proud of their accomplishments in this early space race, and what better way to commemorate them than with a monument in Moscow? In 1958, the Russians organized a competition, and of the 350 entrants, the one selected—by sculptor Andrei Petrovich Faidysh-Krandievsky (1920–1967) with architects A. N. Kolchin and M. O. Barshch—captures the spirit of these early adventures. The grand dedication of the Monument to the Conquerors of Space was held on 4 October 1964, seven years after the launch of Sputnik I. At the base of the monument is a museum, which opened in 1981, and the complex also contains a sculpture of Russian space pioneer Konstantin Tsiolkovsky.

The monument is situated outside the All-Russia-Exhibition Centre (VDNKh), a type of scientific trade fairground or permanent world's fair of Russian technical achievements that dates back to 1935. The site houses a variety of pavilions, including a reconstruction of the modernist Soviet pavilion from Expo '67 in Montreal, Canada.

? The design team created an amazingly sculpted image of a rocket launch. It was neither abstract like U.S. space monuments such as the Astronaut Memorial (1991) at Cape Canaveral, Florida, nor realistic or at least referential to human form, as are the many sculptures of cosmonaut Yuri Gagarin. However, this dynamic shaft celebrates the drama of the machines as much as the skill of the people who made them. Its sweeping appearance has been copied in smaller monuments and was seen on postage stamps and propaganda posters as well as prints throughout the socialist world in the 1960s and 1970s.

We realize, of course, that the triumph of our space conquerors is a feat of the entire Soviet people, a victory for the entire socialist camp.

NIKITA KHRUSHCHEV

Abstract commemorative structures such as this provided a Western counterpoint in modernist design during the Cold War (1948–1989) between the United States and the Soviet Union, compared with some large-scale Russian monuments that were historicist in appearance.

GATEWAY ARCH
EERO SAARINEN
1965

When Eero Saarinen (1910–1961) entered the competition to design this monument in 1947 he had no large buildings to his credit. He had collaborated previously with his father, architect Eliel Saarinen, and together they had won the competition in 1945 to build the General Motors Technical Center (1956) in Warren, Michigan. This became Eero's first really large commission as lead architect. The Gateway Arch in St. Louis, Missouri, or officially the Jefferson National Expansion Memorial, was planned in 1947 but not finished until 1965, and it marks both the beginning and culmination of his career. The arch commemorates the westward expansion of the nation. As a clean-lined symbol of U.S. pioneering spirit, it also seems like an abstraction of a space launch. The memorial project began as a 1930s Depression-era idea for riverfront urban renewal, proposed by St. Louis civic leaders and the federal government. Established by presidential executive order in 1935, a 91-acre (37-ha) site was cleared of slum buildings but the historic courthouse (1861) and old cathedral (1834) were saved. Citizens raised funds for an architectural competition in 1947, and of the 172 entries Saarinen's inverted catenary curve was selected. Funding difficulties delayed completion until 1965, and the arch did not open until 1967. It has been a National Historic Landmark since 1987.

The stainless steel-clad structure is the tallest monument in the United States, at 630 feet (192 m) high. An internal tram in each side has eight egg-shaped pods that seat five passengers. They ascend within four minutes to an enclosed observation deck.

Of his design, Saarinen said that he wished to '. . . create a monument which would have lasting significance and would be a landmark of our time. . . . Neither an obelisk nor a rectangular box nor a dome seemed right on this site or for this purpose. But here, at the edge of the Mississippi River, a great arch did seem right'. He conceived the arch to be perfect in its architectural form and its symbolism. The competition judges liked the design because its dramatic curve framed the dome of the historic courthouse and the cathedral.

Despite the threat of fines and pilot licence revocation, ten pilots have flown small airplanes through the arch since 1966.

Dulles International Airport, 1962, Eero Saarinen
Dulles, VA, USA

HOUSTON ASTRODOME
HERMON LLOYD AND W. B. MORGAN
1965

Hermon Lloyd (1909–1989) and W. B. Morgan (1906–1962) were modernist architects in postwar Houston, known for commercial buildings and the stadium at Rice University (1950). Their Houston Astrodome was built to house the city's new baseball team, the Houston Astros, and many residents consider the building to be their city's equivalent of New York's Empire State Building (1931). When the Astrodome was constructed at the height of the space race between the United States and the Soviet Union, it became a symbol of that competition, more so than the official buildings that Charles Luckman designed for Houston's Manned Spacecraft Center (1963). Groundkeepers at the stadium wore promotional astronaut outfits, waitresses in the Countdown Cafeteria were called Blast-off Girls, fans could buy souvenirs in the Galaxie Gift Shop and the club's marketing proclaimed the stadium to be the eighth wonder of the world. Architecturally, the Astrodome—built to seat 46,000—was the forerunner of major concrete-domed stadia in the United States during the 1960s and 1970s. However, the stadium was replaced by a new one downtown in 2000, and since then residents have unsuccessfully sought an adaptive reuse of this major landmark.

The reinforced concrete stadium is eighteen storeys high and its dome measures 710 feet (220 m) in diameter and 208 feet (63 m) high. When players complained of glare from the skylights, the glass was subsequently painted. This impacted on the grass field, which was re-covered in 1966 with a synthetic grass, renamed Astroturf after its installation here. The stadium held its last baseball game in 1999.

The University of Illinois Assembly Hall (1963) by Max Abramovitz was the first domed concrete stadium. Others followed, but most have been demolished, except the Superdome in New Orleans (1975).

SkyDome, 1989,
Rod Robbie
Toronto, Canada

After Hurricane Katrina (2005), the Astrodome was used as a shelter for some 25,000 evacuees from New Orleans.

Astros president Roy Hofheinz cited the Colosseum (80 CE) in Rome as a conceptual model for the Astrodome. The air-conditioned domed stadium was designed to overcome excessive heat, humidity and rain in cities such as Houston, which might lead to the cancellation of baseball games. Other covered arenas followed, but a movement in the 1990s heralded a return to open-air stadia of nostalgic design.

Unlike the large formal exhibition domes of steel and glazed panels, geodesic domed houses often have more individualized construction, maintenance, heating, ventilation and planning problems than their rectilinear counterparts. These include difficulties in subdividing spaces within and constructing polygonal domes using milled timber.

U.S. PAVILION EXPO '67

RICHARD BUCKMINSTER FULLER

1967

Richard Buckminster (Bucky) Fuller (1895–1983) was a visionary inventor who has been credited with more than twenty-eight patents, including one for the geodesic dome dated 29 June 1954. The geodesic dome is a structure in which lightweight polygonal facets are placed in tension with one another, distributing stresses throughout the framework. During the Cold War (1948–1989) between the United States and the Soviet Union, World's Fairs presented opportunities for rival superpowers to showcase national inventions and technology. In 1967, the choice of Fuller's twenty-storey geodesic dome—200 feet (62 m) high and 250 feet (76 m) in diameter—for the U.S. Pavilion in Montreal demonstrated great technical superiority. It housed six storeys of exhibits designed by the young architectural firm Cambridge Seven Associates. After the fair, the welded steel building could not be disassembled easily so it remained in Montreal as a gift from the United States. Its acrylic panels melted in a fire in 1976, but the dome was reconstructed in 1995 by Eric Gauthier, and converted into the Montreal Biosphere Environment Museum.

The Climatron, 1960,
Thomas Howard
St. Louis, MO, USA

Spaceship Earth, 1982,
Walt Disney Imagineering
Epcot, FL, USA

Long Island Green Dome, 2005,
Kevin Shea Baiting Hollow,
New York, NY, USA

In the late 1920s, Fuller had invented similar polygonal-faceted tensile structures termed 'Dymaxion'—an acronym of 'dynamic', 'maximum' and 'tension'. He redesigned the Dymaxion house in 1945 and one of these later variants is reconstructed in the Henry Ford Museum (1929) in Dearborn, Michigan.

The well-connected Fuller was a natural to design the U.S. Pavilion at Expo '67. Previously he had designed smaller geodesic domes for U.S. government agencies, including the U.S. Pavilion (1956) at the Jeshyn Fair, Afghanistan, and radar installations for Distant Early Warning sites (1957). These latter radomes are so strong that they can withstand winds up to 180 miles per hour (289 kph). More than 300,000 geodesic domes have been constructed worldwide. The largest glazed geodesic dome since 'Bucky's Bubble' at Expo '67 is a thirteen-storey one at Henry Doorly Zoo (2002) in Omaha, Nebraska.

The television tower was intended as a symbol of Berlin and the strength of East Germany. Although Henselmann had proposed the broadcast tower in a sketch made in 1958, it was not until 1964 that communist party chairman Walter Ulbricht authorized its construction. Ulbricht was a supporter of this kind of project, as he was both a science proponent and an avowed opponent of West Germany.

Television Tower, 1956, Heinle, Wischer and Partner Stuttgart, Germany

CN Tower, 1976, John Andrews Toronto, Canada

Henselmann and Streitparth designed the tower, and it was refined by Fritz Dieter, Günter Franke and Werner Ahrendt. The concrete-clad steel shaft contains two lifts and a steel staircase. Made of prefabricated sections and clad in stainless steel, the sphere is 105 feet (32 m) in diameter and weighs 4,800 tons.

TELEVISION TOWER

HERMANN
HENSELMANN AND
JÖRG STREITPARTH

1969

Like skyscrapers, television towers were socio-political statements and tourist attractions. The earliest was built in Stuttgart, West Germany, in 1956. It soars to 711 feet (217 m) and inspired an intercity rivalry with Dortmund (1959), Munich (1972) and Frankfurt (1979). Naturally, East Germany responded tit-for-tat. The Television Tower (Fernsehturm) in Berlin was originally 1,196 feet (365 m) high, and with its gigantic Sputnik-like ball housing a restaurant and observation deck it was taller than the Stuttgart tower. Influential architect Hermann Henselmann (1905–1995) conceived the idea and collaborated with Jörg Streitparth. The base has a plaza with a solar system fountain and a Urania world clock. After the reunification of Germany in 1990, the tower was renovated and a new antenna installed, which increased its height to 1,207 feet (368 m).

The tower was nicknamed Telespargel (teleasparagus), in response to its form, and the Pope's Revenge because of the cross-like shadow it cast over the new communist plaza.

After the war, Henselmann practised a historicist style popular in the Eastern Bloc under Joseph Stalin, but with Nikita Khrushchev's rise to power in 1953, modernist buildings achieved popularity again. Henselmann's later modernist works include the City-Hochhaus, Leipzig, and the JenTower, Jena (both 1972).

"

I am attracted to free-flowing sensual curves . . . in the mountains of my country . . . and on the body of the beloved woman.

? In 1956 President Kubitschek told Niemeyer: 'Oscar, this time we are going to build the capital of Brazil.' Niemeyer designed the presidential residence, various government buildings and the cathedral. Although he was an avowed atheist, he modelled the hyperboloid columns after an image of outstretched praying hands.

When a military dictatorship replaced a democracy in the 1960s, Niemeyer fled Brazil for Paris and did not return to his homeland until 1985. He continued to design poetically expressive, curvilinear structures and was awarded the Pritzker Architecture Prize in 1988.

CATHEDRAL OF BRASÍLIA

OSCAR NIEMEYER

1970

Oscar Niemeyer (1907–2012) is considered to be a pioneer of South American modernism. After training in Rio de Janeiro, he worked with Lúcio Costa in the 1930s, and both architects strove to bring a regional variant of European modernism to Brazil. Niemeyer worked on Costa's Ministry of Education and Health (1943) in Rio and on the Brazilian Pavilion at the New York World's Fair in 1939. After World War II, he was an important part of the team that helped design the United Nations Headquarters in New York (1952). However, the key to Niemeyer's success was his Pampulha entertainment complex (1943), which he built for Juscelino Kubitschek, who later became president of Brazil and offered Niemeyer the chance to design the new capital of Brasília (1956). The dynamic cathedral was part of this plan. Work began in 1958, and the actual structure was completed in 1960. However, Kubitschek's presidency ended in 1961, and many of the Brasília buildings remained unfinished when construction stalled. Although the project was funded by the government originally, the Catholic Church finished the cathedral in 1970. The adjacent oval baptistery was dedicated in 1977, and the complex became a national monument in 1990. It was restored in 2012.

Niterói Contemporary Art Museum, 1996, Oscar Niemeyer
Niterói, Brazil

Oscar Niemeyer Museum, 2002, Oscar Niemeyer
Curitiba, Brazil

Sixteen curved concrete columns form a hyperboloid structure 230 feet (70 m) in diameter and 138 feet (42 m) high. In this, columns curve inwards rather than outwards as in a barrel. The cathedral roof is fibreglass infill between the concrete columns, with stained glass by Marianne Peretti suspended beneath. The light-filled space is accessed by an entrance tunnel from the plaza.

? With its dynamic escalators, Terminal 1 evokes excitement and movement much like the visitor escalator ascent at the Centre Georges Pompidou (1977). Andreu's subsequent work is comparable in both efficiency of planning and dramatic design. His expansions at Roissy in Terminal 2 (1972–2008) were curved variants of linear plans, which enabled easy access and fast check-in gates for passengers.

CHARLES DE GAULLE AIRPORT TERMINAL 1
PAUL ANDREU
1974

Paul Andreu (1938–) has impacted globally on buildings for commercial aviation more than any other architect. Having earned a civil engineering degree from Ecole Nationale des Ponts et Chaussées (1963) and an architectural one from Ecole Nationale Supérieure des Beaux-Arts (1968), he has spent most of his career working for Aéroports de Paris (ADP). From the jet age of the early 1960s to the wide-body airliners of the 1970s, commercial aviation boomed internationally. Orly International Airport (1961) in Paris was intended to be a new jet-age facility, but passenger demand and increasingly larger airplanes, such as the Boeing 747, fuelled the planning and design of a purpose-built airport on a rural site some 12 miles (19 km) northeast of Paris at Roissy. Terminal 1 was Andreu's first major design. Begun in 1967 and completed in 1974, the new airport was named after the French president, Charles de Gaulle. The project led to Andreu being commissioned to design and consult on other ADP expansions at both Roissy and Orly, as well as at airports in Bordeaux, Dubai, Osaka, Manila, Nice, Santiago and Shanghai. He also received additional large-scale commissions after his work on La Grande Arche de la Défense (1989) in Paris. These included Osaka Maritime Museum (2000), Grand National Theatre (2008) in Beijing and Grand Theatre (2013) in Jinan, China.

Centrally planned airport terminals date back to the cylindrical Gatwick Airport (1936) in London. In anticipation of increased traffic and passenger loads, other centrally planned terminals, sometimes with people-moving systems to connect them, were built in Kansas City (1972), Toronto (1972) and Berlin (1974).

Centre Georges Pompidou,
1977, Renzo Piano and Richard Rogers
Paris, France

Interiors of the Renaissance Center, 1977,
John Portman
Detroit, MI, USA

The futuristic interiors of Terminal 1 can be seen in feature films such as *The Concorde . . . Airport '79* (1979), the last of the *Airport* series of films, in which a chase scene takes place on the maze of escalators.

Terminal 1 is a nine-storey cylindrical building—a concrete doughnut—connected to seven satellite buildings by underground passages. The satellites contain the actual gates, and the main building's centre is crisscrossed by glazed escalators. The centralization of landside functions, such as parking and check-in, away from airside ones resulted in a concentration of volume, twice the size of Orly International Airport, that could accommodate increased passenger numbers.

 The conceptual precursor to this multifunctional school space was the Floraskin (1971) project, an expanding biomorphic hotel that remains unbuilt. Fortunately the School Hall gave Domenig a chance to give tangible form to the organic ideas that he and Huth had developed for Floraskin. Another driving force behind the building was the school's art teacher, Sister Irmentraut König, whose interest in contemporary art was fuelled by Graz's art festival, held since 1968.

The atmosphere is free . . . and progressive. They do not stumble under the cultural burden of Vienna.

 T-Centre, 2004, Günther Domenig Vienna, Austria

**SCHOOL HALL
GÜNTHER DOMENIG
1977**

Günther Domenig (1934–2012) was often considered to be an outsider in Austrian architecture during the 1970s, before it was fashionable to be regarded as such. He studied architecture at the University of Technology in Graz in the 1950s, and worked with Eilfried Huth from 1963 to 1973. Throughout his career, Domenig was seen as the leader of the so-called Graz school of architecture, whose design philosophy was not inhibited by the historical references that surrounded his architectural colleagues in Vienna. One of his best-known commissions is Zentralsparkasse Bank (1979) in Vienna. It resembles a giant alien or insect, whose smiling mouth opens wide to welcome customers into its lobby. Domenig created other expressive buildings including his own home (2008), a concrete, steel and glass building near Klagenfurt. He designed it to relate to the nearby mountain landscape, but it projects a mechanistic image that recalls the *Transformers* films (2007–). Domenig's multipurpose School Hall in Graz, designed with Volker Giencke, is the vanguard of all his amazingly independent architectural creations, constructed within a school building run by nuns.

Before Floraskin in Morocco, Domenig and Huth worked on more straightforward projects in Austria, such as the concrete buildings of the Pedagogic Academy (1969) in Graz and the similarly styled Parish Centre (1969) in Oberwart.

Functioning as a dining hall and multifunctional space for students, the building is approximately 200 feet (61 m) long, with its curved tail connecting to the corner of the court, and 80 feet (24 m) wide. The arched steel structure with steel netting is covered in sprayed concrete, 3 inches (8 cm) thick, that was originally painted white. In 1987, a rolled covering of titanium zinc called RHEINZINK® was set atop it, under Domenig's direction, for weatherproofing.

The unusual eight-storey steel, glass and stucco building appears as a contemporary Baroque monument within an historic district. It has an entrance facade with dramatically curved intertwining towers, nicknamed Fred and Ginger in homage to 1930s Hollywood dancers Fred Astaire and Ginger Rogers. The bent towers are a tangible expression of the ideas of both Gehry and Milunic to create a building that represents static and dynamic forces.

The bent towers perhaps represent the new Czech Republic's transition from a socialist state to a democracy.

**DANCING HOUSE
FRANK GEHRY
1996**

Canadian-born Frank Gehry (1929–) exploded onto the international stage in 1997 with his Guggenheim Museum Bilbao, Spain, which became the epitome of what is known as Deconstructivist architecture: buildings in which angular planes and structure appear to be irrationally designed, essentially making a conscious visual effort to break out of the proverbial box. The worldwide hype about Guggenheim Museum Bilbao made Gehry an international 'starchitect', but it also overshadowed some of his other buildings that are equally important. His first large structure was the angular Aerospace Museum of California (1984), in which inverted cantilevered walls create a large exhibition space within. This early building led to the swirling mass of the Vitra Design Museum (1989) in Weil am Rhein, Germany, and the stacked curves and angular planes of the glazed Weisman Art Museum (1993) at the University of Minnesota. These buildings laid the design groundwork for the Dancing House, also known as the Fred and Ginger building, in Prague, built for the Nationale-Nederlanden Bank. The bank's sponsorship of the project changed its intended use from a cultural one to an office facility.

Architecture should speak for its time and place, but yearn for timelessness.

Gehry's buildings are renowned for their wild shapes, facilitated by the architect's adaptation of CATIA software, developed in 1977 by French aircraft manufacturer Dassault. The Dancing House was Gehry's first to be completely designed with this program. Although the building's appearance remains controversial, the program enabled Gehry to create a contemporary design akin to expressive styles of the past, from Viennese Secession to Art Nouveau.

 Der Neue Zollhof, 1999, Frank Gehry Dusseldorf, Germany

DZ Bank, 2000, Frank Gehry Berlin, Germany

? Czech president Václav Havel promoted this site for cultural use and arranged for Czech architect Vlado Milunic to investigate a building there. When Nationale-Nederlanden Bank became involved, they wanted Milunic to include a high-profile architect, and this led to Gehry. The Dancing House is the result of their collaboration. Its scale, vertical composition and visually distorted facade foreshadow Gehry's later vertical buildings, from the small-scaled Stata Center at the Massachusetts Institute of Technology (2004) to the mega high-rise 8 Spruce Street (2011) in New York.

The skin is of aluminium semi-monocoque construction and like an eggshell or boat hull it takes most of the load. Pendennis Shipyard prefabricated the shell and assembled it onsite. Laminated glass is angled at 25 degrees to prevent reflections onto the playing field.

LORD'S MEDIA CENTRE
FUTURE SYSTEMS
1999

Even those who are not sports fans know that Lord's is a cricket ground in London, but they might not know that it can trace its history back to the 19th century. The current viewing stands have been mostly reconstructed or renovated by well-known architects such as Michael Hopkins and Nicholas Grimshaw. The oldest is the landmark pavilion (1890) designed by Thomas Verity, which has also recently been restored. With this historic context in mind, the Media Centre designed by Future Systems looks as if a spaceship landed on the stands: a giant alien eye observing the interaction of humans on the field. Based in London, Future Systems was founded in 1979 by Jan Kaplický and David Nixon, but the latter left for California in 1980, where he eventually established a practice in design for space travel. The firm created the fantastic Media Centre (now known as J. P. Morgan Media Centre) as a futuristic building for sports reporters. When finished, it was awarded the prestigious Stirling Prize by the Royal Institute of British Architects.

Selfridges, 2003,
Future Systems
Birmingham, UK

Future Systems created a number of conceptual designs in the 1980s for system-built structures. The Media Centre is an outgrowth of those plans combined with Nixon's design work for NASA in the same era.

Wooden monocoque construction was first developed in airplane design by Swiss aviator Emile Ruchonnet in 1911.

The intention was to add a state of the art structure to the historic Lord's site that would herald the new millennium. Future Systems fulfilled the brief and for the International Cricket Council's World Cup in 1999 created a futuristic look that put the club on the map for years to come. It led to other large commissions, including the undulating Selfridges store in Birmingham (2003) and a new building for the National Library of the Czech Republic in Prague (2007; unexecuted).

> If that first idea is good then you are on the right track. It's not a sign of creativity to have sixty-five ideas for one problem, that's just a waste of energy.
>
> JAN KAPLICKÝ

Gehry began experimenting with computer software programs in the early 1990s to help visualize complex three-dimensional surfaces. He used an adaptation of the complex CATIA software to help build his enormous fish sculpture—180 feet long (55 m) and 115 feet (35 m) high—for the Barcelona Olympic Games in 1992.

EXPERIENCE MUSIC PROJECT FRANK GEHRY 2000

If the Guggenheim Museum Bilbao (1997) by Frank Gehry (1929–) created an international frenzy after its completion, the architect's equally important, very creatively designed Experience Music Project in Seattle became notorious to many as the 'world's ugliest building'. Critics unfairly described it as 'haemorrhoids', 'the blob' and 'something that crawled out of the sea, rolled over, and died'. The $250 million project was the brainchild of Microsoft cofounder Paul Allen, developed with his sister, Jody Allen. It provided one of the earliest fully interactive museums, and the exhibitions were designed by Seattle's LMN Architects, who were also Gehry's associates on the job. At its core, the museum houses the Jimi Hendrix collection, and it also focuses on rock and roll from the 1960s and 1970s to Seattle's grunge music years of the 1990s. The interior features a concert venue for 800 with state of the art electronics, including a giant high-definition LED screen. The Science Fiction Museum and Hall of Fame were added in 2004, and the nonprofit institution was rebranded in 2013 as the EMP Museum, with a focus on popular culture.

Graceland, 1939,
Furbringer &
Ehrman
Nashville,
TN, USA

*American Jazz
Museum*, 1997,
Gould, Evans,
Goodman
Associates
Kansas City,
MO, USA

The concrete-and-steel building is clad in 3,000 panels, with 21,000 stainless steel and aluminium shards in gold, silver, red, blue and 'purple haze'. Gehry rearranged pieces of broken guitars to create the effect. He also used computer-aided design, such as computer-milled panels. The ultimate in urban interaction, the Monorail from the Century 21 Exposition in 1962 travels through the museum.

The clients wanted a building that projected '...the energy of self-expression through music and culture, and a visitor experience that starts before you walk into the building'. Jody convinced Paul to commission an interactive museum where the public could have an immersive experience related to the artefacts. She wanted an environment that represented the creativity of rock music. They contracted Gehry while the Guggenheim Museum Bilbao was under construction.

I figure this building isn't going to wreck Seattle. If it turns out like the model, we have a chance to make something special.

The £52 million facility has three basic structures: one for temporary exhibits; one for permanent exhibits, with a planetarium built on a former stormwater tank; and the third, a distinguishing bulbous rocket hall, for housing Thor and Blue Streak missiles. This has a steel skeleton 138 feet (42 m) high, covered by inflated ethylene tetrafluoroethylene bubbles similar to those Grimshaw used in Eden's domes. This skin is self-cleaning, and its individual cushions are easily replaced if damaged. Additional materials are concrete and stainless steel for the tower's core.

National Aquatics Centre 'Water Cube', 2008,
PTW Architects
Beijing, China

NATIONAL SPACE CENTRE
NICHOLAS GRIMSHAW
2001

The family-friendly National Space Centre in Leicester, England, gets A+ ratings from visitors for its artefacts, interactive exhibits and educational programmes. What makes the experience even better is the otherworldly framework that Nicholas Grimshaw (1939–) created for the facility. After training at the Architectural Association School of Architecture, he worked with Terry Farrell until he started his own firm in 1980. Coming from an engineering-orientated family, Grimshaw is probably best known for his beautifully detailed steel-and-glass buildings that are informed by industrial-era cast fittings. Perhaps the most striking is the addition to Waterloo Station in London: the gracefully arched, streamlined International Terminal (1993) houses two storeys of passenger facilities. Its success led to other buildings in England, Berlin, Bilbao and Frankfurt, among other cities, as well as the bus shelters for New York City. The Eden Project (2001) in Cornwall, England, was the most adventurous, and its bulbous forms were designed concurrently with those in the National Space Centre. The latter projects the image of an alien-like habitat but it also recalls the extensive experimentation that architects and engineers have performed on inflatable buildings for space travel.

You get a satisfaction out of seeing that detail and you feel you're in the presence of something rather grand. . . .

NASA experimented with inflatable habitats for space colonization in the 1960s. A more recent example is TransHab, an inflatable Kevlar®-armoured fabric construction that could be used as a space station module and for travel to Mars. TransHab was created by architect Kriss Kennedy with Constance Adams and others at the Johnson Space Center, Houston.

Widespread media attention on the Eden Project—an environmental family attraction begun in 1998—may have influenced the selection of Grimshaw's competition entry in 1996 to design a comparable science-based attraction in Leicester. His design created flexible space and energy-saving options, and reused existing foundations and structures in a model of sustainability for this brownfield site.

? At first glance, this anthropomorphic design of mostly fibreglass-reinforced concrete may seem at odds with its location. Yet the architect strove to have the building's fluidity relate to the landscape and contrast with the rectilinear urban forms that surround it. The layered folds of the building seamlessly integrate with the plaza, taking Hadid's work to the next level of sophistication in digital design.

HEYDAR ALIYEV CENTRE
ZAHA HADID
2012

Zaha Hadid (1950–) stated, 'There are 360 degrees, so why stick to one?' This explains in part her openness to experimentation beyond utilizing standard geometric forms. She has also spoken about the complexities of future society, as represented in the sci-fi thriller *Blade Runner* (1982), and how her own designs explore these complexities. This positive approach to experimental design and planning—easier nowadays with computer-aided design programs—helps to explain many of her dynamic projects, including the Heydar Aliyev Centre in Baku, named after the first president of an independent Azerbaijan. Hadid began design of the project with a competition entry in 2007, and five years later the building was inaugurated. The 619,000-square-foot (57,519 sq m) complex features an undulating concrete roof and wall structure that not only relates to the natural topography but also defines exhibition and performance spaces within. Its overall appearance was intended to make a distinct contrast with the rectilinear blocks of earlier Soviet-era architecture, and to express the optimistic future of Azerbaijan, in a way similar to that of expressive contemporary works in Baku, such as the Crystal Hall (2012) by GMP, Flame Towers (2012) by HOK and SOCAR Tower (2013) by Heerim Architects.

Computer-aided design techniques received a huge boost in the late 1990s, especially with Frank Gehry's use of CATIA software, which was developed originally for the aerospace industry. Today, there are several dozen design programs that help architects create dynamic structures. Zaha Hadid's office uses Autodesk® Maya® and a CATIA product from Gehry Technologies to transform design dreams into buildable realities.

>

I have always appreciated those who dare to experiment with materials and proportions.

Hadid's early works were classified as Deconstructivist, distinctly angular rather than rectilinear, in the spirit of 1920s Soviet Constructivism. Her recent works are boldly curvilinear, and some of the more surprising ones are small structures, such as the shell-like Burnham Pavilion in Chicago's Millennium Park (2009) and the tent-like Serpentine Sackler Gallery (2013) in London.

Catholic Church of the Transfiguration, 2009, DOS Architects
Lagos, Nigeria

Aquatics Centre, 2012, Zaha Hadid Architects
London, UK

The proSolve 370e system is installed in a double wall across 27,000 square feet (2,510 sq m) of the main steel-and-glass facade. Each tile is a heat-formed plastic shell coated with pollution-absorbing titanium dioxide. When pollutants encounter the tiles they are neutralized, changing emissions into carbon dioxide and water. The distinctive shape creates aerodynamic drag that slows wind in order to capture pollutants, and also to better capture light to help photo-catalyze pollutants.

Dring and Schwaag employed natural forms such as the omni-directional structure of sea coral to inform the design of their proSolve 370e tile units.

Enex 100 at St. George's Terrace, 2009,
COX Australia
Perth, Australia

Suspended Screens,
Al Bustan Complex, 2013,
Habtoor Leighton Group
Abu Dhabi, UAE

TORRE DE ESPECIALIDADES
ELEGANT EMBELLISHMENTS
2013

Climate change, carbon fuels and resultant air pollution are all increasingly disturbing phenomena within our society, which has witnessed efforts to go green on a variety of levels. Allison Dring (1974–) and Daniel Schwaag (1972–) of the Berlin-based firm Elegant Embellishments, founded in 2008, are seeking new responses to these issues when it comes to building design and materials. Dring's interdisciplinary experience includes work with a variety of London firms, such as Urban Salon Architects and Pentagram, whereas Schwaag has a background in computer-generated design and worked extensively with Arup Associates. Although they have exhibited their works internationally, their major contribution to the environment in terms of architecture is the development of proSolve 370e, a decorative facade tile that also neutralizes air pollution within urban environments. They first demonstrated the product on a large scale in the new hospital building, Torre de Especialidades, in the Tlalpan neighbourhood of Mexico City. Although not actually tested, the tiles have a life expectancy of pollution absorption of five to ten years, and after that they will require recoating. On the hospital facade, the tile screen negates the pollution of some 1,000 cars per day.

Others are investigating building materials that are grown and harvested. Examples include bioMASON, a firm that uses bacteria to bind cement to an aggregate that hardens into bricks, and Philip Ross, whose mycelium bricks are made from mushrooms. David Benjamin used the latter to build the four-storey Hy-Fi Mushroom Tower (2014) in New York.

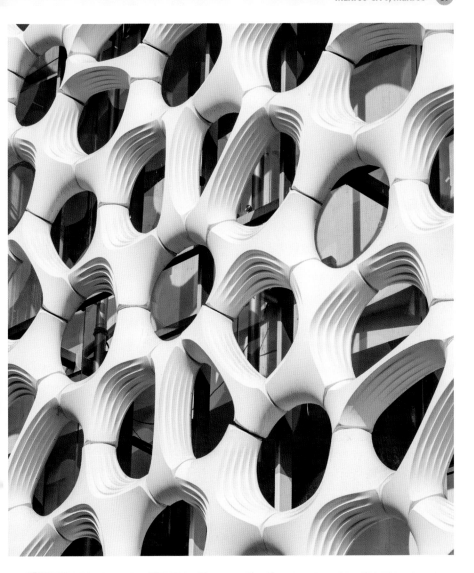

Mexico City's air quality leaves much to be desired. Elegant Embellishments' use of a pollution-negating tile—often nicknamed 'smog-eating'—was intended to be 'visibly apparent to the public'. The architects see it as a model for other applications on urban structures that have bland or blank facades, such as parking garages, although its use before this hospital facade was within decorative interior components.

KING FAHD NATIONAL LIBRARY
GERBER ARCHITEKTEN
2013

German-born and trained Eckhard Gerber (1938–) started his own architectural office after graduating from Technische Hochschule in Braunschweig in 1966. His current firm, Gerber Architekten, dates from 1979, and since then he has taught at the universities of Essen and Wuppertal. The firm of 120 employees, in Berlin, Dortmund and Hamburg, realizes projects mostly across Germany and more recently in Saudi Arabia.

If Gerber and his design colleagues have a style it is classical modernist, often working in steel and glass to create mostly rectilinear constructions with universal spaces within. He has been referred to as a socially progressive architect who, as a teenage refugee from East Germany, values democracy and freedom and sees himself as an emissary of those values to other societies when he works outside Germany. His firm's philosophy is to analyze the site, history and socio-cultural context in order to provide a rational design solution and create an architectural expression of the client: the building acting as a tangible logo or symbol. The King Fahd National Library in Riyadh, Saudi Arabia, is a creative remodelling and expansion of an earlier library structure; the new facade not only projects a dynamic image for the building but also relates to imagery within Saudi society.

Stadthalle, 1981,
Gerber Architekten
Hagen, Germany

*Chemistry Institute,
University of Giessen*, 2014,
Gerber Architekten
Giessen, Germany

Fabric-roofed structures made of Kevlar® and other blends, along with coatings of polytetrafluoroethylene (PTFE), date back to Curt Fentress's Denver International Airport (1995) and Helmut Jahn's Munich Airport Centre (1999). PTFE tension roofs can also be found atop stadia worldwide; one of the most notable is Berlin's Olympic Stadium (1936), renovated in 2004.

Thomas Lücking, Gerber's design director, likened the fabric-covered facade to the Bedouin tent tradition and veils, stating: 'To cover and veil precious objects in Saudi Arabia is also a tradition.'

The prominence of Gerber's Göttingen State and University Library (1993) led to an invitation to compete for this job. His design of a fabric-animated facade was successful because it referenced the importance of veils and the tradition of nomadic tents within Saudi society. More than that, Gerber created a universal structure in which the separate spaces for men and women within—typical of Saudi society today—are adaptable to societal changes in the future.

 This library renovation surrounded the extant building with a steel-and-glass structure on each side, creating an addition that encapsulates the original marble structure. With Riyadh temperatures sometimes surpassing 110°F (43°C), the firm created a steel cable-supported fabric skin of 1,000 PTFE sails. These animate the building and also act as a sunscreen.

 In my opinion, architecture still receives insufficient attention and is attributed too little cultural worth.

ECKHARD GERBER

Foster's spaceport recalls his curved, hangar-like, prefabricated concrete American Air Museum (1997), with a dash of alien overtones in its undulating concrete form. The design seeks to encompass both the mysterious and the thrilling aspects of space travel. The facility is a first of its kind, and other architects have already begun to design spaceports for sites in Texas and Colorado.

American Air Museum, 1997, Norman Foster Duxford, UK

Canary Wharf Underground Station, 1999, Norman Foster London, UK

The thin-shelled concrete terminal building has large glazed windows overlooking the field and runway. The facility is designed to achieve LEED Platinum status, with the terminal partly bermed into the landscape, thus taking advantage of natural ventilation and geothermal energy.

**SPACEPORT AMERICA
NORMAN FOSTER
2014**

Aerospace history was made on 21 June 2004, when *SpaceShipOne* made its maiden flight to orbit as the first privately funded spacecraft. The success of the space flight led Sir Richard Branson to form a partnership with Scaled Composites to create a commercial fleet of Virgin Galactic spacecraft, each of which will take six passengers into orbit. Norman Foster (1935–) and structural engineering firm URS Corporation (in collaboration with SMPC Architects) were selected by the New Mexico Spaceport Authority to design the first commercial spaceport. As an aviation enthusiast and pilot, as well as the architect for Stansted (London, 1991) and Hong Kong (1998) airports, Foster was a natural choice to design this facility. Although Virgin Galactic's first orbital flights have yet to take place, more than 400 space tourists have reserved seats for the $250,000 flight.

When a Pan Am spaceliner appeared in *2001: A Space Odyssey* (1968) it caused a stir, prompting the airline to sign up some 93,000 members in its first moon flight club.

Foster's intention to convey the excitement of space travel with a dynamic form is similar to that of Eero Saarinen when he created the TWA Terminal (1962) in New York in the early jet age. Hangars are scaled to the six-passenger spacecraft to give people the same intimacy they had at the dawn of commercial aviation.

CHAPTER THREE
MAKING A STATEMENT

Popular culture reached new heights in the second half of the 20th century, epitomized in the United States by the fast food and entertainment industries. A collaboration between client and architect established McDonald's trademark 'golden arches' in the 1950s, and the franchise spread both nationally and internationally. In the 1980s, as part of a major revamp programme, Disney hired 'starchitects' to design company buildings, resorts and theme parks. Beyond these industries, this chapter also presents examples of high art designs that have become iconic worldwide. They include Sydney Opera House by Jørn Utzon and the Vietnam Veterans Memorial by Maya Lin. Fine artist Friedensreich Hundertwasser sought a more human architecture in his Waldspirale, and Curt Fentress paid homage to sculptor Felix de Weldon with the National Museum of the Marine Corps.

❮ 'Basket' Headquarters, Newark, Ohio, USA

Goff used his wartime experience in the creative recycling of materials as the stepping stone to his next level of architecture, in examples such as the angular rough-stone Joe Price House (1956), Bartlesville, Oklahoma. Criticisms of his individualistic buildings, teaching methods and lifestyle supposedly led Goff to state, 'There is no such thing as a bastard material or a bastard style. There are only bastard architects.' Locals say that neighbours reacted negatively to the Ford house while it was under construction, and the Fords placed a sign outside responding, 'We don't like your house either,' commenting on the pedestrian nature of more traditional suburban homes.

Like the Ruth Ford House, one of Goff's best-known buildings—the Bavinger House (1955) in Norman, Oklahoma—also uses recycled materials. It was built around a spiral plan from discarded glass slag pieces and local sandstone that the owner dynamited from a large natural rock formation.

RUTH FORD HOUSE
BRUCE GOFF
1949

Bruce Goff (1904–1982) found the path to his own organic style during World War II when he served in the construction battalion of the U.S. Navy in Alaska and California. While in Alaska, he familiarized himself with prefabricated Quonset hut design and construction, and at Camp Parks, California, he executed surprisingly modern spaces within standardized military barracks, including the modern Lounge and Star Bar (1944) and the McGann Memorial Chapel (1945), the latter created from Quonset huts. After being discharged in 1945, Goff designed affordable housing for the Stran-Steel company, again using Quonset huts. He then moved to the Midwest to design the Ruth Ford House in Aurora, Illinois. Using surplus building materials such as Quonset hut ribs, Plexiglas® observation domes from Boeing B-17 bombers and recycled nautical rope for the ceiling patterns, he created a centrally planned living, dining and exhibition space with quarter-circular adjacent spaces for bedrooms and bathrooms. The exterior walls consist of coal and green glass set in mortar that includes children's marbles.

Monte-Silo, 2006, Gigaplex Design Woodland, UT, USA

Villa Welpeloo, 2012, Jan Jongert and Jeroen Bergsma Enschede, The Netherlands

Although 'green' initiatives are typical of the 21st century, they were considered by earlier generations. Contemporary with Goff's Ruth Ford House, Frank Lloyd Wright designed an early passive solar home: the second Jacobs House (1948) in Middleton, Wisconsin. Its convex masonry walls partly buried within a landscape berm face north, whereas the curved solar hemicycle glass facade faces south to warm the living and dining rooms.

Entrepreneur Fred Harvey developed what were arguably the first chain restaurants in the United States in 1875. Called Harvey House lunch rooms, they followed stops on the Atchison, Topeka and Santa Fe railroad lines, and were immortalized in the film *The Harvey Girls* (1946), starring Judy Garland.

McDONALD'S DRIVE-IN
STANLEY MESTON
1955

The United States is often considered the birthplace of fast-food chain restaurants with standardized architectural design. In the 20th century there were many. They include drive-ins such as White Castle, founded in 1921 in Kansas, and White Tower, founded in 1926 in Wisconsin, as well as earlier self-service urban equivalents for office workers. The best known are Horn & Hardart Automats, first built in 1902 in Philadelphia, and the John R. Thompson eateries of the early 1900s in Chicago. The latter were almost all planned by luxury hotel architect Benjamin H. Marshall, who used standardized design and materials, and the same contractors to provide economical solutions nationwide. These buildings paved the way for the success of suburban and urban McDonald's, which even today are characterized by their trademark 'golden arches' logo. In 1952 brothers Richard and Maurice McDonald selected Stanley Meston (1910–1992) to create a new building for their hamburger restaurant. They suggested an arch symbol to make the restaurant more eye-catching. Meston developed the idea with his assistant, Charles Fish, and came up with twin arches that framed the small kitchen structure. Ray Kroc was brought in in 1954 to franchise these restaurants nationally, and within a decade there were more than 700.

Neon-lit, porcelain-clad arches and red-and-white tile construction were used for the small building of less than 900 square feet (83 sq m). In 1985 a reconstruction of the 1955 building in Des Plaines, Illinois, was built next to the actual site and now serves as a museum.

The arch was a brilliant symbol to alert motorists approaching the eatery, and the scale and position of Meston's parabolic arches were simple and effective. The steel arches paralleled the gigantic arch that Eero Saarinen had successfully submitted in 1947 for the Gateway Arch competition in St. Louis. McDonald's original mascot appeared under an arched neon sign in continuation of the theme. Although the physical arch structures were no longer used after the 1960s, the golden arches continue as the McDonald's logo.

Hamburger University was founded in 1961 in Elk Grove Village, Illinois, to train franchisees, each receiving a Bachelor of Hamburgerology degree.

White Castle Prefabricated Building No. 8, 1936, L. W. Ray
Minneapolis, MN, USA

Louis Naidorf of Welton Becket Associates has been credited with the actual design of the building. It immediately became linked with the image of stacked vinyl disks, appropriate for a record company's headquarters. However, Naidorf was unaware of the client's identity, and his intention was to design a functional plan. In it, most offices have a window at the perimeter and the core has lifts, stairs and toilets.

CAPITOL RECORDS BUILDING
WELTON BECKET
1956

Welton Becket (1902–1969) was one of several Los Angeles-based mid-century modernists who shaped the city that we see today. Seattle-born Becket studied architecture at the University of Washington, graduating in 1927. He moved to Los Angeles in 1933 and formed a partnership with Charles Plummer and Walter Wurdeman. Their best-known works include the Moderne Pan-Pacific Auditorium (1935) and homes for film stars James Cagney and Robert Montgomery. After Plummer's death in 1939, Becket and Wurdeman continued to work together, designing buildings such as the streamlined Bullock's department store (1944) in Pasadena. With Becket already established as one of Los Angeles's prominent architects, his firm was a natural choice to design a corporate headquarters for Capitol Records, shortly after Capitol was acquired by British record company EMI. The building has become as much of an icon for Los Angeles as the renowned 'Hollywood' sign. It has also been integral to music history in the United States, because it houses recording studios engineered by Les Paul that have been used by stars from Frank Sinatra to Nat King Cole. Buildings such as Capitol Records are often termed Googie style (coined in 1952) in recognition of the futuristic, atomic-age modernism of the era, particularly popular in southern California.

The thirteen-storey concrete building is 90 feet (27 m) in diameter and 150 feet (46 m) high in order to conform to zoning restrictions. At the top is an executive floor. Becket's firm added sunscreens to the original tower design. The underground sound studios have wood panels that can rotate to fibreglass, depending on acoustical needs. The tower was said to be earthquake resistant, but a recent excavation nearby revealed a seismic fault that has delayed the construction of two large apartment towers that would flank this landmark.

Beverly Hilton, 1953,
Welton Becket
Los Angeles, CA, USA
Gateway West Building, 1963,
Welton Becket
Los Angeles, CA, USA

Capitol Records is often cited as the world's first circular office building. Circular design plans for high-rises were in other architects' minds in that era, from I. M. Pei's proposal for the Hyperboloid in New York (1956) to Bertrand Goldberg's studies for Motel 66 (1958) and the iconic Marina Towers (1964) in Chicago.

The aviation warning beacon on top of the tower blinks out the word 'Hollywood' in Morse code in an example of subliminal messaging.

The jury was enthusiastic about Utzon's initial studies but for practical reasons he replaced the original elliptical shell concept with one based on regular spherical sections, analogous in his mind to the peeling of an orange. When a variety of problems led to Utzon's resignation, architect Peter Hall completed the glazing and interiors. Despite this, Utzon achieved international recognition and was awarded the Pritzker Architecture Prize in 2003. Sydney Opera House was named a UNESCO World Heritage Site in 2007.

Lutheran Church, 1976, Jørn Utzon
Bagsværd, Denmark

National Assembly Building, 1985, Jørn Utzon
Kuwait City, Kuwait

The highest of the precast concrete panel shells is equivalent in height to a twenty-two-storey building. The exterior is covered with a chevron pattern of more than 1 million white and cream-coloured tiles as well as pink granite panels. The interiors are Australian white birch plywood.

SYDNEY OPERA HOUSE
JØRN UTZON
1973

Everyone knows that the Sydney Opera House is an architectural icon of the city, and it catapulted architect Jørn Utzon (1918–2008) to international recognition well beyond his native Denmark. After World War II, Utzon travelled across Europe and to the United States and Mexico to see buildings by Alvar Aalto and Frank Lloyd Wright, as well as ancient Mayan pyramids. He won the competition to build the Sydney Opera House in 1957, which brought him to Australia. Construction started in 1959 but he soon encountered roof design problems, political antagonism from a new government, and an attempt to coerce him into using certain building suppliers. He resigned from the project in 1966 and returned home. Although not invited to the building's grand opening in 1973, Utzon was asked to redesign the reception hall, renamed the Utzon Room (2004), and afterwards renovated other parts of the structure.

In 1960, while Sydney Opera House was under construction, U.S. singer and actor Paul Robeson sung 'Ol' Man River' from atop the scaffolding to construction workers who were taking their lunch break.

Controversy and hostility surrounded Utzon's resignation and left Hall unfairly reviled for taking over the project. Hall worked on other institutional buildings, including co-designing Goldstein College, University of New South Wales (1964).

 Tigerman felt that his buildings were too serious. The erotic design of this home, when seen in the street or from above, was intended to cheer up the terminally ill client, who owned a number of burlesque houses in south Florida. According to Tigerman, the beachfront facade of Daisy House, with Spanish Mission-style overtones, has windows 'winking and blinking at girls on the beach. . . .' The phallic aerial view of the home might also be '. . . cause for low-flying airplanes to crash'.

Richard Meier does Richard Meier; Peter Eisenman does Peter Eisenman. I never felt the need to develop a style.

 Self-Park Garage,
60 East Lake Street, 1986,
Stanley Tigerman
Chicago, IL, USA

DAISY HOUSE
STANLEY TIGERMAN
1978

Many consider Stanley Tigerman (1930–) to be the *enfant terrible* of Chicago architecture but this characterization misses the mark. His works range from mid 1960s multifamily housing in Chicago to polytechnics in Bangladesh, and from the Pacific Garden Mission (2007) in Chicago to the Illinois Holocaust Museum and Education Center (2009) in Skokie. Tigerman has also made equally notable contributions to architectural activism: a sense of morality and ethics, exemplified by his cofounding of Archeworks (1994), a think tank for social good in design. The 1970s were watershed years in the architect's career. He was integral to the revisionist 'Chicago Architects' (1976) exhibition; was a founder of the Chicago Seven postmodern architects movement; and was key to the re-establishment of the pluralistic Chicago Architectural Club (1979). The 1970s also witnessed his ironic sense of humour in individualistic designs. When Mr and Mrs Walter Daisy commissioned Tigerman to build their house in Porter, Indiana, they may not have been sure exactly what they were getting but they knew that no one else would have one like it.

The 3,600-square-foot (334-sq-m) house has cedar cladding facing the street and stucco facing the dunes. The public spaces are in the centre with bedrooms flanking them. Unfortunately, later homeowners changed the natural tone to teal with a white trim.

Tigerman's buildings contain inside jokes often inspired by the clients. This probably began with the Hot Dog House (1975), named from the plan form, in Harvard, Illinois. Others include the Anti-Cruelty Society of Chicago building (1981), which looks more like a neighbourhood than a public building. The main facade has a pedimented entrance with a dog-food can opener atop and cutouts shaped like dogs' ears. Tigerman's self-park garage in Chicago (1986) has a facade modelled on a stylized Rolls Royce radiator.

The concrete structure clad mostly with aluminium and glass is twenty storeys high and measures 300 feet (91 m) long by 37 feet (11 m) wide. There is also a 37 by 37-foot (11 x 11-m) void that holds a swimming pool. As if pulled out of that red and yellow void, the yellow cube below houses a health club.

ATLANTIS
ARQUITECTONICA
1982

The Miami firm Arquitectonica was founded in 1977 by the husband and wife team Bernardo Fort-Brescia (1951–) and Laurinda Spear (1950–) along with Hervin Romney, who left the firm in 1984. Their work is characterized by steel-and-glass modernism, in which facades are sometimes disrupted by voids or geometric forms that animate the buildings. Atlantis's sleekness was punctuated by highlights of colour and form, making it a symbol of 1980s Miami. Prominently featured in the opening clip of the popular television show *Miami Vice* (1984–1990), it became a building associated with new wave music, glamorous women and hip lifestyles. This high-rise condominium set the stage for Arquitectonica's later success in residential projects such as the curved glass towers of Bentley Bay (2005) and the arch-like 500 Brickell (2008), both in Miami.

Arquitectonica had established itself as an apartment house designer firm in Miami before it received this commission, having built the waterfront Babylon (1977) and Palace (1981). Atlantis came on the scene at the right time and received a Progressive Architecture Award (1980) before it was finished.

Laurinda Spear designs products, from furniture to wristwatches to an autographed Acme rollerball with multiple inscriptions of 'the pen is mightier than the sword'.

? Atlantis relates to Miami's Art Moderne designs of the 1930s and the flashy 1950s hotels created by Morris Lapidus, particularly the sleekly curved modernist facade of the Fontainebleau Hotel (1954). Arquitectonica therefore not only established a link to popular precedents but also set a new modern standard for high-rises in Miami. Atlantis's association with *Miami Vice* helped raise national exposure of the building.

MiMA, 2011, Arquitectonica New York, NY, USA

Regalia Miami Condominium, 2013, Arquitectonica Sunny Isle, FL, USA

The competition required an apolitical statement that would contain the names of the dead and also harmonize with the landscape of the 2-acre (0.8-ha) site. Lin's V-shaped memorial wall represents a wound within the park, its almost black glossy surface reflecting the foliage. One commentator also observed that the simple angular shape represents the single stripe rank of an average soldier, a private first class, thereby democratizing the memorial further.

I deliberately did not read anything about the Vietnam War because I felt the politics of the war eclipsed what happened to the veterans. The politics were irrelevant to what this memorial was.

The polished black granite was brought in from Bangalore, India, and each of the two walls is 246 feet (75 m) long. The 57,661 names were inscribed by computerized process in the sequence in which they died. As of 2011, additional inscriptions total 58,272.

VIETNAM VETERANS MEMORIAL
MAYA LIN
1982

Of U.S. and perhaps even international war memorials, the Vietnam Veterans Memorial in Washington, D.C., may well be the most potent in terms of visual impact, especially since it has been replicated in at least two versions that tour across the United States. It commemorates not only those who died but also those who were reported missing in action during U.S. involvement in the Vietnam War (1964–1975). In 1981, while still an undergraduate at Yale University, Maya Lin (1959–) was selected to design the memorial. Lin's intention was for the etched, polished surfaces of the black granite to serve as 'pages in a book of names'. She acted as design consultant to architects Cooper-Lecky Partnership, and the project catapulted her to national acclaim. Subsequent works include the Civil Rights Memorial (1989) in Montgomery, Alabama; the environmental sculpture Ecliptic (2001) in Grand Rapids, Michigan; and Langston Hughes Library (1999) and Riggio-Lynch Chapel (2004), both in Clinton, Tennessee.

Holocaust Memorial, 2004,
Peter Eisenman
Berlin, Germany

Personal items left at the memorial are archived in the Vietnam Veterans Memorial Collection, established in 1986.

Washington's Korean War Veterans Memorial (1995) and National World War II Memorial (2004) were more conservatively designed, perhaps as a reaction to the abstract Vietnam memorial.

? Johnson's blocky vertical mass, with its highly decorated top and a profusion of decoration at the lower-level grand entrances and lobby, was built in the tradition of skyscrapers from the early 1900s. For some, the grandly arched lobby was reminiscent of the Galleria (1877) in Milan. When the AT+T Building opened in 1984, it soon became the epitome of a postmodern skyscraper, and was often compared with Michael Graves's pink granite Humana Building (1985) with loggia in Louisville, Kentucky, and KPF's 900 North Michigan Avenue (1989) in Chicago, Illinois, clad in cream-coloured limestone and green glass.

"

. . . painters have every advantage over us today. Besides being able to tear up their failures—we never can seem to grow ivy fast enough—their materials cost them nothing.

AT+T BUILDING
PHILIP JOHNSON
1984

Ludwig Mies van der Rohe said, 'A chair is a very difficult object. A skyscraper is almost easier. That is why Chippendale is famous.' Mies's protégé Philip Johnson (1906–2005) certainly knew this when he designed the AT+T (now Sony) Building in New York City. Although the tower was both revered and reviled in the press, it catapulted the architect to the cover of *Time* magazine. Earlier in his career, in the 1930s, Johnson's years as a curator and journalist were linked by two extremes: promoting avant-garde European modernism in the landmark exhibition 'The International Style: Architecture Since 1922' (1932) and promoting the German army's *Blitzkrieg* successes in Poland and France for the right-wing magazine *Social Justice* (1939–1940). After a brief stint in the U.S. Army during World War II, Johnson studied architecture at Harvard, graduating in 1943. His postwar career included the design of his own minimalist Glass House (1949) in Connecticut, and the interiors of Mies's Seagram Building (1958) in New York. His own firm, established in 1967 with John Burgee, became known for historically contextual buildings, from the Gothic glass PPG Place (1984) in Pittsburgh to 190 South LaSalle Street (1987) in Chicago, created as a Romanesque Revival homage to U.S. architect John Wellborn Root.

Johnson's work is often considered in terms of postmodernism. Earlier buildings, however, show his sensitivity to history. Notable among these are the Italian Renaissance-inspired Amon Carter Museum (1961) in Fort Worth, Texas; the Renaissance piazza at New York's Lincoln Center (1964), modelled on the Piazza del Campidoglio in Rome; and the Art Museum of South Texas (1972) in Corpus Christi, its poured concrete walls and tower evoking Spanish Mission-style architecture.

Humana Building, 1985, Michael Graves
Louisville, KY, USA

900 North Michigan Avenue, 1989, KPF
Chicago, IL, USA

The thirty-seven-storey tower is 647 feet (197 m) high and clad in pink granite. When AT+T moved into the building, Johnson persuaded them to display their *Spirit of Communication* statue (1916) in the lobby; the sculpture was removed when the company left the building in 1992. The lobby galleries were renovated into Sony entertainment experiences in 1994.

The Chetrit Group bought the building from Sony in 2013 and intends to convert part of the structure into ninety-six luxury residences, with Sony continuing to rent office space.

Clark bought this 22-acre (9-ha) site on Pacific View Drive as a retreat from the city below. However, its situation next to Santa Monica Mountains National Recreation Area came with building restrictions and objections from local conservancies that inhibited normal home construction. Brown overcame these by creating a home that appears to be a natural rock formation in the landscape. He was inspired by Frederick Kiesler's sculptural *Endless House,* developed over several decades from the 1920s to the 1950s.

Dick Clark Home, 1982,
Phillip Jon Brown
Pacific Coast Highway, Malibu,
CA, USA

Contractors referred to the house as 'Bedrock', after *The Flintstones* television series (1960–1966).

FLINTSTONE HOUSE
PHILLIP JON BROWN
1988

Architect Phillip Jon Brown (1940–) created this small but distinctive getaway home for entertainer Dick Clark, dubbed the 'world's oldest teenager' and best known as the celebrity host of *American Bandstand* from 1956 to 1989. The weekend home overlooking Malibu, with panoramic views of the Pacific Ocean, Los Angeles and Boney Mountain, was the second house that Brown designed for the Clarks: the earlier one was their main home of almost 10,000 square feet (929 sq m) on the waterfront Pacific Coast Highway, completed in 1982. Born in Columbus, Ohio, and raised in California, Brown earned his first degree in architecture from the University of Southern California and a master's degree from Massachusetts Institute of Technology. He then returned to Los Angeles, where he set up his own architectural practice in 1973. Over the past four decades, Brown has developed a speciality in creating custom-designed homes. He has also continued a passion for urban design and transportation issues, proposing a Flow Boulevard system to alleviate Los Angeles's notorious traffic problems.

Although this house is unique, the Mushroom House (1972) in New York is similarly styled. Designed by James H. Johnson, it was constructed using concrete poured within excavated earth forms, and the finished pods were lifted atop concrete pylons.

This small one-bedroom, one-bathroom home of 2,300 square feet (214 sq m) is constructed of wood and steel beams, covered in thick coloured stucco on mesh. A local aggregate within the stucco was washed to reveal the stones. Because of the building's unique construction, Brown built much of the Flintstone House himself along with the interior fittings. Standard cabinets were resurfaced with moulded urethane foam and fibreglass to create rock-like drawers and doors.

The mostly wood-frame house stands near a cliff overlooking the Pacific Ocean. The clients wanted the building to relate to the waves below, so Prince designed its undulating roof shingles that also appear within. Built around a central court, the interiors curve into one another, becoming a single free-form surface. Including an addition built in 1996, the entire structure occupies 4,500 square feet (418 sq m).

> *There should be as many individual designs as there are individual people.*

PRICE RESIDENCE
BART PRINCE
1989

Known locally as the mushroom house, this individualistic building projects an almost sci-fi image from its driveway entrance at the end of a cul-de-sac in Corona del Mar, California. This impact is even more pronounced because the Price Residence, although quite private, is surrounded by homes that look as if they belong on U.S. television shows set in suburbia, such as *Knots Landing* (1979–1993) and *Desperate Housewives* (2004–2012). The keyword here is 'individualist' because it best describes both the architect, Bart Prince (1947–), and the clients, Joe and Etsuko Price. Prince worked as an assistant to inventive U.S. architect Bruce Goff, and his buildings are an extension of his mentor's individualistic attitude towards creating distinctive homes. Beyond Goff, Prince acknowledges the importance of architects Frank Lloyd Wright and Antoni Gaudí as well as other creatives such as Albert Einstein, Pablo Picasso and Claude Debussy. Prince's work is different for each client yet all the buildings have a look of stubborn design independence from popular norms of today. One of his clients, Steve Skilken, saw the Price Residence and 'thought it was spectacular', which confirmed his interest to commission Prince to design his own home. The Prices' home and grounds also include an authentic Japanese teahouse.

Borden/Wiegner Residence,
1998,
Bart Prince
Jemez, NM, USA

Steve Skilken Residence, 1999,
Bart Prince
Columbus, OH, USA

Although Prince is known for designing large-scale homes for affluent individuals, he also produced the multifamily Parsifal Townhomes (2004) in Albuquerque, New Mexico. He employed the same high standards of construction to produce twenty-four affordable residences.

As a major collector and donor to the Los Angeles County Museum of Art, Joe Price worked with Goff on the design of the institution's pavilion for Japanese art in 1978. Prince finished the museum building, as Goff's assistant, in 1988. With both Prince and Price as the keepers of Goff's legacy, it is natural that they would work together on Price's own home, which is also used as a study centre for his Japanese art.

**TEAM DISNEY
BURBANK
MICHAEL GRAVES
1991**

Walt Disney created an entertainment empire unlike any seen before within the film, theatre, television and amusement park industries. The company that he founded in 1923 with his brother, Roy, has today more than 175,000 employees and revenues of more than $45 billion. Led by chief executive Michael Eisner from 1984 to 2005, Disney was revitalized and expanded in a number of ways. This included hiring 'starchitects' to design buildings at studio headquarters and in Disney resorts and theme parks. Major league designers in the 1980s and 1990s working for Disney included Frank Gehry, Aldo Rossi, Robert A.M. Stern, Robert Venturi, and Arata Isozaki, the last of whom designed the first Team Disney building (1990) in Florida. In 1986 Eisner oversaw Disney's corporate restructuring, in which the company renovated and expanded facilities at its famed studios in Burbank, California, originally built in 1940. Michael Graves (1934–2015) was commissioned to design the Team Disney office building and Robert A.M. Stern the Feature Animation Building (1994). The former contains sculptural references to the seven dwarfs because the Burbank studios were originally built with the profits from the film *Snow White and the Seven Dwarfs* (1937), whereas the latter has a pointed sorcerer's cap referencing Mickey Mouse's hat in the film *Fantasia* (1940).

Walt Disney's first cartoon character was Mickey Mouse, created in 1928. He made his debut in *Steamboat Willie* and was an instant success.

It has been observed that Walt's nephew, Roy E. Disney, was not happy with this building and used it as an example of what needed to change within the company. Roy resigned from the board in 2003 and, in part, led a faction to replace Disney's leadership. Although Eisner resigned in 2005, this Team Disney headquarters was renamed for him in 2006.

Team Disney Orlando, 1990, Arata Isozaki
Lake Buena Vista, FL, USA

Team Disney Anaheim, 1995, Frank Gehry
Anaheim, CA, USA

Disney Office Complex, 1994, Aldo Rossi
Orlando, FL, USA

? Graves created this postmodern version of a classical temple as an homage to *Snow White and the Seven Dwarfs*. He had been at the peak of his career in the 1980s, with major buildings such as the Portland Building (1982) in Oregon and the Humana Building (1985) in Louisville, Kentucky. He was therefore a natural choice for Eisner, who saw merit in hiring high-profile architects who would increase the exposure of the very media-conscious Disney empire.

The red sandstone and stucco office building of 350,000 square feet (32,516 sq m) is approached via a trellised plaza. The facade recalls the Parthenon (438 BCE) in Athens, and each of the sculpted dwarfs holding up the pediment is more than 19 feet (6 m) high. Atop is a rotunda, which houses the corporate dining room with Mickey Mouse motifs.

I want you to make me smile, because I know I'm going to have an extraordinarily difficult day.

MICHAEL EISNER
TO MICHAEL GRAVES

The thirty-storey, 364-foot-high (111-m) glass hotel cost $375 million to build and originally housed 2,526 rooms along with a 100,000-square-foot (9,300-sq m) casino. The interior featured a giant pyramidal atrium of 29 million cubic feet (820,000 cu m). When the resort opened, it included a Nile River ride and a reduced size replica of the Great Sphinx. Inside there was a King Tut tomb and a museum, as well as Egyptiana throughout. Renovated in 2009, the hotel now has 4,400 rooms and a 120,000-square-foot (11,148-sq m) casino.

LUXOR HOTEL
VELDON SIMPSON AND CHARLES SILVERMAN
1993

Advertising copy such as 'What happens in Vegas stays in Vegas' harkens back to the 1950s: an era in which casinos in Las Vegas projected the image of Sin City. This changed in the 1980s and 1990s, when the city's casinos offered not only adult-orientated activities but also family-friendly ones, akin to themed amusement parks. Some even had dedicated kid zones, separate from the cavernous gambling floor. Combining a themed environment with casino functions enabled hoteliers to create giant complexes, with thousands of hotel rooms, that provided guests with an exotic yet safe escape from the mundane world. For most Americans, a trip to the themed New York-New York Hotel & Casino (1997) or the Paris Las Vegas Hotel & Casino (1999) is less intimidating than actually visiting those cities. Some cite Caesar's Palace (1966), with its Roman environment, as the first themed hotel; others regard the Mirage (1989) as the pioneer of the fantasy escape resort. However, the first overtly historically themed mega resorts were the Gothic Excalibur Hotel (1990) and the Egyptian Luxor Hotel (1993)—architectural environments that were consistently styled, inside and out. Both were the work of Veldon Simpson (1941–) and Charles Silverman (1933–).

The Korvelo Group offers a pyramid home design that is resistant to earthquakes, hurricanes, tsunamis and tornadoes.

All casinos have the same product to offer.... But you would rather go into something that is adventurous than just plain vanilla.

CHARLES SILVERMAN

Other pyramidal buildings include the high-rise office Transamerica Pyramid (1972) in San Francisco and the Rainforest (1993), Discovery (1997) and Aquarium (1999) pyramids at Moody Gardens in Galveston, Texas. Because of the connotations of exotica and eternity in this Egyptian form, some private homes have been built as curiosities, such as the Gold Pyramid house in Wadsworth, Illinois (1977).

? Nevada architect Simpson and southern California interior designer Silverman of Yates-Silverman—veterans in resort, hotel and entertainment design—created a spectacularly consistent and well-detailed piece of Egyptian Revival architecture in the Luxor Hotel. When the hotel opened, its pyramid made it the tallest building in Las Vegas and its exterior was arguably the most recognizable. Simpson and Silverman had previously worked together to create the medieval-styled Excalibur Hotel next door.

Transamerica Pyramid, 1972, William Pereira
San Francisco, CA, USA

Pyramids at Moody Gardens, 1993–1999, Studio Red with Morris Architects
Galveston, TX, USA

Seattle-based NBBJ is known for big projects, and its Columbus office was headed by Friedrich K.M. Böhm when the 'basket' was constructed. He remarked: 'It's a piece of Pop art . . . elegant but not kitschy—and it could have gotten kitschy very easily.'

'BASKET' HEADQUARTERS
NBBJ
1997

Architectural follies that represent animals or objects date back to the 19th century and earlier. These range from Lucy the Elephant (1882) in Atlantic City, New Jersey, used as a real estate office, to supersized products, such as the Dole Pineapple Water Tower (1927) in Hawaii; the demolished Radio Flyer wagon pavilion at the 1933 Chicago World's Fair; the hot dog-shaped Wienermobile (1936) used to advertise Oscar Meyer food products; and the Haines Shoe House (1948) in Hellam, Pennsylvania. The 'Basket' Headquarters comes out of that tradition in which buildings and machines serve as product advertisements. Dave Longaberger founded his company in 1976 to manufacture and supply handmade wooden party baskets. His idea for the headquarters building was inspired by a group of employees who created what was then the world's largest basket—48 feet (14 m) long by 23 feet (7 m) high—as a marketing display for the Ohio State Fair in 1980. The basket is a permanent attraction in Dresden, Ohio, where Longaberger was founded. This set the stage for the Longaberger 'Basket' Headquarters in Newark, Ohio, designed by architectural firm NBBJ.

The stucco-covered steel building is 192 feet (58 m) long and 126 feet (38 m) wide, but tapers upwards to 208 feet (63 m) by 142 feet (43 m). It houses office space for some 500 employees, a seven-storey atrium and a 142-seat auditorium. The basket handles are made of 300-foot (91-m) pieces of galvanized steel that include a heating element to melt winter ice. Two Longaberger gold-leaf tags are attached to the sides of the building.

Team Disney Burbank, 1991, Michael Graves Burbank, CA, USA

Feature Animation Building, 1994, Robert A.M. Stern Burbank, CA, USA

Longaberger pushed the architects to create a true basket building and not simply a steel-and-glass structure slightly decorated with basketry. He used the company's Medium Market Basket for the architects' model. With NBBJ he created what the *Wall Street Journal* claimed was a marketer's dream brought to life, and it brings bus loads of basket collectors each year to tour the building.

They can put a man on the moon and bring his butt back, and . . . we can't construct a building that looks like a basket?

DAVE LONGABERGER

The twelve-storey concrete, stucco and tile building has 105 apartments and a restaurant within one of its turrets. Tree plantings make the layered building appear as if it is a part of the landscape. In all, the complex has 1,000 windows; none is like another.

WALDSPIRALE

FRIEDENSREICH HUNDERTWASSER

2000

Born in Vienna, Austrian artist and architect Friedensreich Hundertwasser (1928–2000) most probably never saw a geometrical straight line that he liked, in part because he consistently referenced natural forms within his work. He said: 'The straight line is godless and immoral.' His work as an artist expanded to include the applied arts and architecture, which most likely relates to his environment, in which many postwar Viennese artists and architects harkened back to the city's tradition of highly decorative and expressive works by Secessionists such as Gustav Klimt and Otto Wagner. From the early 1950s Hundertwasser consistently pursued his goal of a more human architecture in harmony with nature. His buildings were executed with architects Peter Pelikan and Heinz M. Springmann, as well as Josef Krawina. The Waldspirale (Forest Spiral) in Darmstadt, Germany, built with Springmann, is an extension of his architecture philosophy outside Vienna.

Springmann also worked with Hundertwasser on lesser-known projects in Germany, such as the remodelling of the Luther-Melanchthon-Gymnasium school (1999) in Wittenberg and the Living Beneath the Rain Tower residential complex (1993) in Plochingen.

Within its public spaces, such as the staircase and corridors, the Hundertwasser House (1986) apartment building in Vienna features undulating floors as if they were part of an irregular landscape.

KunstHausWien, Museum Hundertwasser, 1991, Friedensreich Hundertwasser
Vienna, Austria

Heating Plant Spittelau, 1992, Friedensreich Hundertwasser
Vienna, Austria

? Hundertwasser integrates trees, uneven floors, afforestation of the roofs and spontaneous vegetation to achieve harmony with nature. The colourful stucco and gilt organic form of Waldspirale is typical of his work, but why here? Like Vienna, Darmstadt has its own Art Nouveau landmarks, the most notable of which is Mathildenhöhe artists' colony (1899) designed by leading German and Austrian architects of the era. It also has a significant Russian Chapel (1899), and its onion domes are referenced in the Waldspirale.

Outdoor weddings with water backdrops are popular all over the world. Perhaps the best-known Japanese site for these is the *torii* gate at the 16th-century Itsukushima Shrine in Hatsukaichi. It seemingly floats at high tide and provides a spectacular backdrop for traditional weddings.

LEAF CHAPEL
KLEIN DYTHAM
2004

Weddings are big business, and hotels host services as well as receptions for them. The Japanese in particular have created a series of chapels at resort hotels dedicated to wedding ceremonies. Renowned architect Tadao Ando created a spectacular one known as Chapel on the Water (1988) in Tomamu, Japan, and Klein Dytham's striking little Leaf Chapel in Kobuchizawa is part of that tradition. Astrid Klein (1962–) and Mark Dytham (1964–) established their Tokyo firm in 1991. Since then they have created dynamic projects, particularly in retail and media, such as the Wonder Room (2007) in Selfridges, London; the prototype Sony Store (2011) first built in Los Angeles; and the YouTube Space (2013) in Roppongi, Tokyo. Perhaps their biggest contribution to culture worldwide is the creation of PechaKucha Night in 2003: it is an opportunity for young designers to showcase their work in twenty images over twenty seconds each, an event that is replicated in more than 680 cities internationally.

The tiny steel chapel sits within a hotel garden adjacent to a *koi* pond. When the veil is closed, glazed panels above the structure illuminate the space. The curving steel-panelled veil opens at the ceremony's end, allowing the bride and groom to greet guests in the garden. Polycarbonate lenses within the patterned dome illuminate a nylon scrim with leaf patterns. The structure is lightweight and earthquake resistant, and sits on a concrete basement that contains the HVAC systems.

Chapel on the Water, 1988,
Tadao Ando
Tomamu, Japan

White Chapel, Hyatt Regency Hotel, 2006,
Jun Aoki
Osaka, Japan

Hoshino Resorts hired Klein Dytham to create this mechanized wedding chapel. The architects responded to the client's wish for a garden pergola by creating a design based on two leaves. One large leaf is mechanized, recalling the wedding veil being lifted for the couple's kiss, and the leaf perforations illuminate the space within. Happy with the result, the client hired Klein Dytham to reclad its twin forty-storey 1980s hotel towers.

> *[The client] knew we are media savvy and would design something that would attract attention in the magazines.*
>
> MARK DYTHAM

As with many artists, architects and designers, Brown saw his home as his design laboratory, akin to works by like-minded individualists such as Bruce Goff and Bart Prince. Some have said that he learned his attention to craft detailing during his time at Robert A.M. Stern's office. Brown's own home gave him the opportunity to share his knowledge not only with his Cincinnati students but also with other local craftspeople who contributed their time to this expressively individualistic house.

> *Terry believed it was an architect's responsibility to invent solutions for clients that they didn't know were possible.*
>
> LESLIE CLARK, ARCHITECT

An existing small house was drastically remodelled using a host of materials that would not usually be seen in one building. Everything from cedar shingles, copper, ceramic and glitter to plywood, stained glass, sheet metal and tile is used here, all combined in a very personal geometry to create the final effect.

MUSHROOM HOUSE
TERRY BROWN
2006

Terry Brown (1955–2008) earned his first degree in architecture from Iowa State University (1977) and his master's from Washington University in St. Louis (1979). After graduating he worked with a variety of architects who were cutting-edge figures in the late 1970s and 1980s, including Aldo Rossi and Robert A.M. Stern, as well as Venturi, Rauch, and Scott Brown. Each architect had an open attitude towards contextualism and historic forms, as would be expected from architects who were classified as postmodern. Brown moved to Ohio to teach at the University of Cincinnati (1982–1983) and began his own practice, initially designing contextual homes. However, a Fulbright Fellowship awarded in 1986 enabled him to travel to Vienna and experience firsthand the highly decorated, often gilded works of Viennese Secession buildings, and compare them with North American Prairie School architects of the same era. This changed his life. Upon his return, he started to develop his unique personal style, which found its ultimate expression in his own home—Mushroom House—built in the Hyde Park neighbourhood of Cincinnati with the help of his university students.

Bavinger House,
1955, **Bruce Goff**
Norman, OK, USA

Cosanti, 1956,
Paolo Soleri
Paradise Valley,
AZ, USA

Home and Studio,
1984, **Bart Prince**
Albuquerque,
NM, USA

When Brown visited Vienna on a Fulbright Fellowship in 1986, the work of Secession architect Otto Wagner—Karlsplatz Stadtbahn station and Majolikahaus (both 1899)—dazzled him. These design-detail masterpieces influenced Brown's subsequent efforts to combine decorative elements with the organic forms of some Prairie School architects.

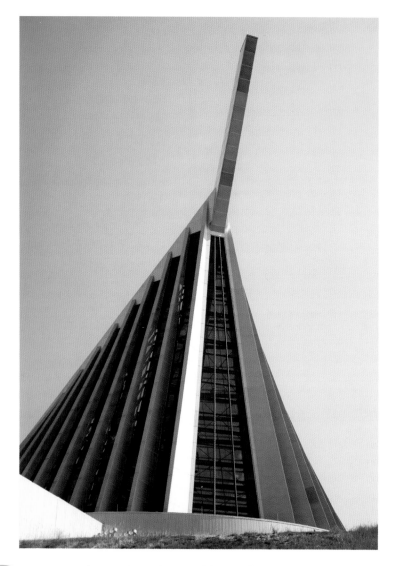

The building's angular geometry intentionally recalls that of the Marine Corps War Memorial (1954) by sculptor Felix de Weldon, who based his work on the iconic photograph of marines raising the U.S. flag at Iwo Jima, taken by Joe Rosenthal in 1945. Fentress intended the museum to be a new icon of the Marine Corps, and his competition entry was selected, in part, because of his experience with large jobs.

NATIONAL MUSEUM OF THE MARINE CORPS
CURTIS FENTRESS
2006

Curtis Fentress (1947–) always wanted to be an architect, even as a toddler making constructions in his sandpit. He was educated at North Carolina State University, and after graduation in 1972 he worked for I. M. Pei and Kohn, Pedersen, Fox (KPF) in New York. There, he immersed himself in many of the large-scale projects realized by both firms. After working on a KPF job in Denver, Fentress branched out on his own and started a partnership with James Henry Bradburn in 1980. Together they tackled large jobs, mostly throughout the American West, until Bradburn's retirement in 2004. The firm garnered a number of great commissions, including Denver International Airport (1995), Incheon International Airport (2001) in South Korea and Invesco Field at Mile High (2001) for the Denver Broncos American football team. Under Fentress alone, successes continued with Arraya Tower (2009) in Kuwait City and airport terminals in Seattle (2005) and Los Angeles (2013 and ongoing). Although Fentress had done some museum work before, the National Museum of the Marine Corps in Triangle, Virginia, was his firm's largest cultural job. More than simply a large museum, it is the centrepiece of a 135-acre (55-ha) Fentress-designed campus that includes a chapel, memorial park, meeting centre and hotel. The chapel was completed in 2009.

Although best known for large projects such as stadia and airports, Fentress has developed a niche market in museum design. One of the first of these was the expansion of the National Cowboy Hall of Fame and Western Heritage Center (1965) in Oklahoma City, but a more striking example is the National Museum of Wildlife Art (1994) in Jackson Hole, Wyoming, a construction of rough-hewn masonry that blends into its rugged setting.

This museum is a new icon. Whether it is Iwo Jima [or] rifles held at ready ... the clean lines and modest materials are suggestive and reflective.

The central steel-and-glass atrium comprises ten storeys and is 210 feet (64 m) high, with two-storey marble walls that have inscriptions related to Marine Corps history. The original building of 118,000 square feet (10,962 sq m) is to be expanded to a total of 200,000 square feet (18,580 sq m).

Bundeswehr Military History Museum extension, 2011, Daniel Libeskind
Dresden, Germany

Imperial War Museum renovation, 2014, Foster + Partners
London, UK

The concrete viewing bowl and steel-banded 'nest' encompasses 2.84 million square feet (202,900 sq m), and its post-Olympic capacity is 80,000 people. The dynamic steel framework wraps around the stadium's form, and its roof structure is filled with ETFE (Teflon®) foil. Reports in 2012 cited the need to repair steel corrosion, especially in welded joints.

BEIJING NATIONAL STADIUM

HERZOG & DE MEURON

2008

Edible birds' nests are considered an iconic delicacy in China, so the nickname 'Bird's Nest' for Beijing National Stadium, built for the Olympic Games in 2008, catapults this distinctive structure to the forefront of Chinese culture. The design is the work of Swiss firm Herzog & de Meuron, founded in 1978, and Li Xinggang of the China Architecture Design and Research Group, with Chinese artist Ai Weiwei as consultant and Arup as engineers. Jacques Herzog (1950–) and Pierre de Meuron (1950–) had already made their mark on the international architectural landscape when they converted Bankside Power Station in London to house the new Tate Modern (2000), which helped them to win the Pritzker Architecture Prize in 2001. Although other museum commissions followed soon after, in San Francisco and Minneapolis (2005), it was the success of the Allianz Arena (2005) in Munich that was the proving ground for the iconic National Stadium in Beijing. Although the centrepiece was seen worldwide during television coverage of the Olympic Games, it is still searching for a permanent use beyond occasional concerts and sporting events. However, thousands of tourists flock to see the Bird's Nest every year and buy souvenirs within the shopping centre at its base.

Winning the Pritzker Architecture Prize supposedly set Herzog & de Meuron on a change of course, from minimalist work to more adventurous designs. The Allianz Arena and Beijing National Stadium fit well within this interpretation.

? Herzog & de Meuron intended the voluminous space to be a 'gigantic collective', one akin to an 'undulating vessel' of comparable scale to those within the acclaimed etchings of grandiose architectural constructions by Giovanni Battista Piranesi. The perimeter design creates a 'chaotic forest' that encompasses the central space. The nickname 'Bird's Nest' was given to this project by the Chinese, although the design detail is the architects' creation.

St. Jakob-Park, 2001, Herzog & de Meuron Basel, Switzerland

❝

Its appearance is pure structure. Facade and structure are identical.

ASPEN ART MUSEUM
SHIGERU BAN
2014

Some people think of Aspen, Colorado, as an upmarket ski resort, peppered with villas owned by celebrities and billionaires. However, others recall the intellectual rebirth of this historic mining town after World War II, epitomized by the think tank Aspen Institute (founded in 1950), offshoot film and music festivals, and design conferences. The Aspen Art Museum relates to both of these overall impressions. Founded in 1979, the original non-collecting museum was located in a former small power plant and focused on exhibitions by local artists. The museum leadership decided to expand the exhibition scope to include well-known contemporary figures from across the nation, and to build a new facility, three times the size of the original. In 2007 the museum selected Japanese architect Shigeru Ban (1957–) to design the building. Previously Ban had achieved acclaim for his creative design solutions for temporary structures after major disasters, including buildings after the Kobe earthquake (1995) and the so-called Cardboard Cathedral (2013) in New Zealand. The commission in Aspen was one of the few instances in which Ban was chosen to build a permanent structure.

This cubic building of 33,000 square feet (3,065 sq m) is a three-storey glazed box covered by a triangular wood roof. Its basket-weave screen, some 47 feet (14 m) high on two facades, is constructed from a composite of paper, wood and resin. Within the building are more traditional, neutral spaces for displaying art. Visitors can take the grand staircase or glazed lift to reach the top, which is open to views of the landscape.

Spanish company Prodema has developed a variety of outdoor and indoor wood products over the past century and more. Its wood- and resin-clad buildings in Oslo and Sydney received awards at the World Architecture Festival in 2014.

Ban wanted to 'open the building to the outside so visitors could appreciate the beauty of Aspen from inside the building', likening the museum's visitor flow from the rooftop foyer to the experience of skiing down a mountain. His distinctive woven facade quickly became a symbol for the museum but also referenced his past work with paper and cardboard as a building material. For some, the basket-weave design offers a visual temptation to climb the building as if it were an urban attraction, which resulted in a police arrest and a fine in October 2014, soon after the museum's opening.

Liberty Place,
2013,
Francis-Jones
Morehen Thorp
Sydney,
Australia

The Carve, 2014,
a-lab
Oslo, Norway

CHAPTER FOUR
SKYSCRAPER STYLE

Skyscrapers continue to capture the public's imagination. This fascination is most probably related to intercity and international rivalries concerning who has the biggest and the best tall tower. In addition to height, architects employ any number of geometric shapes to distinguish their work from that of rivals. Although the modern skyscraper of the 1970s was undoubtedly an American creation—by firms such as Skidmore, Owings & Merrill—in the 21st century European architects including Santiago Calatrava, Norman Foster, Rem Koolhaas and Renzo Piano have challenged this hegemony. Furthermore, many of the designs in this chapter confirm that the high-rises that have been built in recent times are commonly multiuse residential and commercial towers, unlike the skyscraper clubs, skyscraper churches and skyscraper universities of the early 20th century.

❮ The Shard, London, UK

Minoru Yamasaki's World Trade Center in New York (1972; destroyed) briefly held the title of the world's tallest building until the completion of the Sears Tower. New York's One World Trade Center, or Freedom Tower (2014), by Daniel Libeskind and David Childs of SOM, is now the tallest building in the United States, at 1,776 feet (541 m).

> It would be difficult to say with words or music what I feel I can say best with building.
>
> BRUCE J. GRAHAM

One Magnificent Mile, 1983, Skidmore, Owings & Merrill Chicago, IL, USA

The concept of the bundled tube design, in which each tube is a different height, is believed to have been inspired by an open pack of cigarettes.

SEARS TOWER
SKIDMORE, OWINGS & MERRILL
1973

The Sears Tower (now Willis Tower) was the tallest building in the world until 1996, when the Petronas Twin Towers were completed in Kuala Lumpur. It was the culmination of joint efforts by architect Bruce J. Graham (1925–2010) and engineer Fazlur Khan (1929–1982), who worked in the Chicago office of Skidmore, Owings & Merrill (SOM). Peruvian-born Graham joined SOM in 1951 and was made a design partner in 1960. He played a leading role in many of the Chicago office's commercial buildings, from the Inland Steel Building (1958) to the John Hancock Center (1970) and the award-winning One Magnificent Mile (1983), and also some of the firm's exports abroad, such as 135 Bishopsgate and 1 Appold Street (both 1988), and the Canary Wharf master plan (1985), all in London. Graham was the driving force behind SOM securing and constructing these projects; Khan was the engineering genius who made them buildable. Born in Bangladesh, he joined SOM in 1955 and is best known for developing the braced tube design of high-rises, in which the building's perimeter, not its core, is the load-bearing structure. This system was first used in Chicago's DeWitt Chestnut Apartments (1965). Bundled tubes were also utilized in Chicago's One Magnificent Mile and Onterie Center (1986), the latter being Khan's last work, begun in 1979.

The painted, aluminium-clad, steel-frame tower is 108 storeys or 1,451 feet (442 m) high. Its nine bundled, staggered tubes form a square at the base, 225 feet (69 m) on each side. Sears has double-storey spaces on the thirty-third to thirty-fourth and sixty-sixth to sixty-seventh floors for sky lobby lift transfers.

Khan and Graham had previously created a braced single-tube construction in Chicago's John Hancock Center. The Sears Tower comprised a structural system of nine bundled tubes, effectively nine buildings, each supporting one another to a record-breaking height, and each with potentially open space plans. There were to be six additional bundled tubes to accommodate a hotel, but these were never built.

The triangular concrete tower is twenty-seven storeys or 289 feet (88 m) high. It has irregularly spaced 5-inch (12-cm) slit windows—the spacing stipulated for prison bars—and their narrowness eliminated the need for iron bars. Lower floors contain offices and social services, whereas the top sixteen storeys house single-occupancy cells within modules serving forty-four detainees. Each module has a lounge, a kitchenette, and dining and visiting rooms. An exercise yard is atop the skyscraper.

Time-Life Building, 1969,
Harry Weese
Chicago, IL, USA

Swisshôtel, 1989,
Harry Weese
Chicago, IL, USA

During the recession of the mid 1970s, Weese demolished Chicago's Art Deco Diana Court (1929) and replaced it with a concrete Marriott Hotel (1978), in order to prevent laying off employees.

METROPOLITAN CORRECTIONAL CENTER
HARRY WEESE
1975

Harry Weese (1915–1998) was a maverick. When others in the 1960s and 1970s chose design sides, Weese went his own way. He provided clients with modern buildings executed in a variety of materials that sometimes had historic precedents. After training at Massachusetts Institute of Technology, he studied with Finnish architect Eliel Saarinen before establishing his own firm in Chicago in 1941. After naval service in World War II, Weese returned to design practice. Over the next half century, he designed buildings of all types, each of them a unique expression of modern architecture. His first prominent job was the U.S. Embassy (1958) in Ghana, a two-storey office of mahogany and concrete. Other notable works include the simple, almost monastic, brick First Baptist Church (1965) in Columbus, Indiana; the cylindrically modern masonry Seventeenth Church of Christ Scientist (1968) in Chicago; skyscrapers such as the rust- and bronze-toned COR-TEN® steel-and-glass Time-Life Building (1969) in Chicago; and the dramatic, concrete-vaulted spaces of the underground stations (1966–1976) in Washington, D.C., in which the coffers recall grand classical design. The Metropolitan Correctional Center in Chicago, later William J. Campbell Courthouse Annex, is another example of Weese's pioneering individualism.

Weese designed and built several skyscrapers, each unique. They were constructed of different materials and design, from the textured, steel Time-Life Building to the slick aluminium- and glass-clad triangular Swisshôtel (1989), both in Chicago. Weese also planned the world's tallest building in 1982—Chicago World Trade Center—but it was never built.

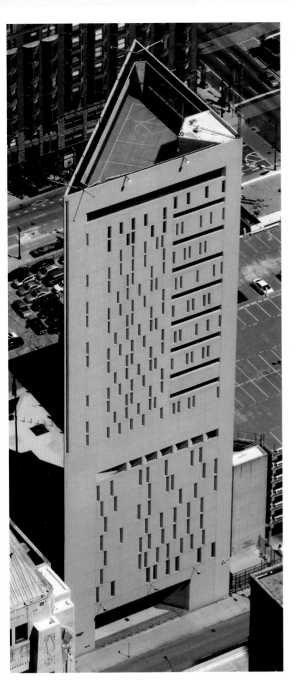

Karel Yasko was one of the chief architects at General Services Administration, and his acquaintance with Weese led to this commission. The prison was intended as a temporary facility for those on trial within Chicago's federal court, and not for long-term incarceration. The programme also stipulated a garage for federal car pool use. Weese solved these problems by creating a high-rise in a triangular footprint, planning the interiors as if he were designing communities within a residential hotel, rather than a dormitory or prison. Although the design was well intentioned, the prison has been said to be overcrowded with both long- and short-term detainees, as is the case in most similar facilities today.

[Architecture is] the discovery of fresh combinations of old ingredients appropriate to present problems.

Kanchanjunga Apartments address Correa's concerns for the local environment and create an Indian modernism with an overall Western appearance. In keeping with India's climate, his design solutions draw on the tradition of residential verandas that act as sunscreens and heat barriers. He also orientated the structure east to west in order to provide city views and to take advantage of ocean breezes.

KANCHANJUNGA APARTMENTS
CHARLES CORREA
1983

Charles Correa (1930–) is an acclaimed pioneer of modernism within his native India. He studied at the University of Bombay and then in the United States at the University of Michigan and Massachusetts Institute of Technology (MIT) during the 1940s and 1950s. He returned to Bombay (now Mumbai) and established his own architectural practice in 1958. Like many mid-century modernists, Correa was influenced by Le Corbusier, especially by the latter's work in planning the city of Chandigarh in the 1950s, and giving India a vision for a new architectural tradition. In 1955 he saw Le Corbusier's Jaoul House in Paris under construction and said: 'It was a whole new world way beyond anything being taught in America at that time.' Correa combined modern form with sensitivity to India's climate and building conditions. These include his 'tube-house' narrow plan for residential commissions, focused on sun shielding and systematic air circulation, developed in 1962 for Ahmedabad's very hot and humid environment. His practice included low-income housing for Bangalore (1972) and Kanchanjunga Apartments in Mumbai. Although many cite his early pioneering work, more recent buildings include the Jawaharlal Nehru Centre (1994) in Bangalore, Salt Lake City Centre (2004) in Kolkata, and MIT Neuroscience Center in Boston (2005).

The twenty-eight-storey reinforced-concrete luxury building contains thirty-two duplex apartments with up to six bedrooms. The apartment plans are comparable with units in Le Corbusier's Unité d'Habitation (1952) in Marseille, France. The building's core was the first use of vertical slipform construction in India. This is where concrete is poured within a continuously moving building formwork at regular intervals after each layer has dried, thus creating strong building cores while minimizing scaffolding and crane use.

Gandhi Smarak Sangrahalaya, 1963, Charles Correa
Ahmedabad, India

Sonmarg Apartments, 1966, Charles Correa
Mumbai, India

Slipform construction was first used in the early 20th century to build silos and grain elevators. It was patented by Chicago engineer James MacDonald in 1917.

The units in Correa's high-rise apartment towers—Sonmarg Apartments (1966) and Kanchanjunga—were planned with India's climate in mind so that primary living spaces are placed away from the terraced, tiled perimeter and secondary spaces such as dressing rooms, bathrooms and studies.

 No one could have foreseen that this tower would take on another function: as a residence for more than 750 families including some 2,500 homeless occupants. This creative reuse of the unfinished building has not helped to secure the tower's future, and it may well be demolished. Residents are said to have been relocated in 2014, and the Venezuelan government is considering the building's fate.

Sathorn Unique Tower, 1997, construction halted, Rangsan & Pansit Bangkok, Thailand

The forty-five-storey, partly glazed concrete structure is 620 feet (190 m) high. Its current use for informal housing saw improvised changes to the building regarding plumbing and electricity. There are no lifts, so residents must climb and descend the high-rise via concrete stairwells.

**TOWER OF DAVID
ENRIQUE GOMEZ
1994**

Economic problems can stop a high-rise in its tracks. When this happens before a project begins, the architectural renderings are unexecuted and often become merely very beautiful dreams. However, there are projects in which the building is halted during construction. These range from a simple hole in the ground, as is the case with Santiago Calatrava's ill-fated Chicago Spire (begun 2007; halted 2008), to towers that are half, or even more, complete. The Tower of David in Caracas, Venezuela, designed by Enrique Gomez, was intended to be a multiuse office building with apartments and a hotel, developed by financier David Brillembourg. Construction was halted by the Venezuelan banking crisis of 1994, and the tower is yet to be finished. It has been occupied by several thousand squatters since 2007 in response to the city's housing crisis.

The Tower of David became a backdrop for scenes in the third season of the television thriller *Homeland* (2011–), in which it was used as both a refuge and a prison.

History is full of projects that stopped midstream. Two of the largest are Albert Speer's German Stadium at Nuremberg, begun in 1937 and halted in 1943, and Paolo Soleri's Arcosanti, a city for 5,000 in the Arizona desert. Construction began in 1970, but the current population numbers only a hundred or so.

PETRONAS TWIN TOWERS
CÉSAR PELLI
1997

With the building booms in Asia and the Middle East gathering pace during the 1990s, the quest was on again to construct the world's tallest building. The last title had been secured by Skidmore, Owings & Merrill's Sears Tower (now Willis Tower) in Chicago some two decades earlier in 1973. Having established his reputation in both the United States and Asia, César Pelli (1926–) was at the forefront of this race. Born in Argentina, the architect trained at the University of Illinois and worked for Eero Saarinen, an early pioneer of Neofuturism, and Victor Gruen, best known for designing shopping centres, before starting his own firm in 1977. His own works included major urban complexes and skyscrapers such as the World Financial Center (1987) in New York, 181 West Madison Street (1990) in Chicago, and One Canada Square (1991) in London. Although all these buildings were tall towers—between forty and fifty storeys—they were nothing in comparison to the Petronas Twin Towers, which are more than twice that height. In some ways, Pelli had his design rehearsal for this task in 1988 to 1990 when he planned the Miglin-Beitler Skyneedle in Chicago, an unexecuted design for the world's tallest building at 125 storeys and 1,999 feet (609 m) high. This design went through extensive planning and municipal approvals before being cancelled due to an economic recession. It set the stage for Pelli designing the eighty-eight-storey postmodern twin skyscrapers in Kuala Lumpur a few years later.

Bank of America, 1992, César Pelli
Charlotte, NC, USA

Gran Torre, 2014, César Pelli
Santiago, Chile

The Council on Tall Buildings and Urban Habitat is the arbiter of the world's tallest buildings. Petronas Twin Towers held the title until 2004, when it was surpassed by Taipei 101, designed by C.Y. Lee. In 2010 Skidmore, Owings & Merrill's Burj Khalifa in Dubai took the crown.

The newly completed towers featured in the climax of the film *Entrapment* (1999), starring Sean Connery.

Built of reinforced concrete bundled tubes and clad with a steel-and-glass facade, the eighty-eight floors are serviced by seventy-eight lifts. A double-deck skybridge connects the towers at the forty-first to forty-second floors.

The desire to reach for the sky runs very deep in our human psyche.

After the Miglin-Beitler Skyneedle experience, Pelli embarked on the design of the Petronas Twin Towers in 1992. The Skyneedle had been informed by spiky Art Moderne towers such as the Chrysler Building (1929) in New York; the towers in Kuala Lumpur were likewise topped with multistorey decorative terminations. These relate to geometric Islamic design in Malaysia, particularly the rotated squares, or Rub el Hizb symbols, that produce the angular zigzag setback tower tops.

The twenty-five-storey, 196-foot-high (60-m) steel-and-glass tower contains seventy housing units along with a service floor for amenities. It features a glazed facade with double walls that circulate air in summer and winter, using principles of passive solar energy. The intelligent facade contributes to a uniform climate year-round. Loggias become garden opportunities for residents. Apartments are open-plan loft design and range from 592 to 1,400 square feet (55–130 sq m).

Apartment Towers 'Wienerberg City', 2004, Coop Himmelb(l)au
Vienna, Austria

Akron Art Museum, 2007, Coop Himmelb(l)au
Akron, OH, USA

SEG APARTMENT TOWER
COOP HIMMELB(L)AU
1998

Viennese firm Coop Himmelb(l)au was founded in 1968 by Wolf D. Prix (1942–) and Helmut Swiczinsky (1944–). They chose the firm name, meaning 'Sky Blue Cooperative', so that it would inform their design intention to create architecture as light and ephemeral as clouds. Both Prix and Swiczinsky studied architecture at Vienna University of Technology and their works have focused on dematerializing notions of structure. The earliest of these are their additions to law offices atop a traditional Viennese building (1988) and to the Funder factory in St. Veit (1989). These set the standard for the so-called Deconstructivist movement during the late 1980s and early 1990s, and featured in the landmark exhibition 'Deconstructivist Architecture' (1988) at the Museum of Modern Art (MoMA). This seemingly irrational disassembly of modernist components was, in part, a reaction to the overtly historicist postmodern buildings of the 1980s. The success of early works and the MoMA exhibition launched Coop Himmelb(l)au's reputation internationally. Since that time it has executed an individualistic version of modernism on various scales, from furniture and exhibition design to apartment towers and museums. The SEG Apartment Tower in Vienna is related to the development of two adjacent housing units in the Alte Donau area.

Coop Himmelb(l)au is not a colour but an idea, of creating architecture with fantasy, as buoyant and variable.

Environmentally conscious high-rises of the 1990s often focused on energy-saving solutions related to glazing. Architects today are going beyond that. Elegant Embellishments has created proSolve 370e, a building tile that absorbs pollution. bioMASON has created bricks grown from bacteria.

The concept was to create two stacked buildings with a sky lobby between them that would contain a mall of sorts with a café, playground and sun deck to be used by all within the building. Distinctively wedge-shaped, the tower reflects the firm's efforts to break out of the box in the 1980s and 1990s. Its more recent works, such as BMW Welt (2007) in Munich, tend to be more anthropomorphic than angular.

The octagonal-planned concrete, steel, aluminium, glass and granite tower cost more than $520 million to build. It is 1,380 feet (420.5 m) high, and its eighty-eight floors are serviced by sixty-one lifts. The tower houses offices in the shaft, shopping and hotel services at its base, and an observation deck on the eighty-eighth floor. The 555-room Hyatt hotel features one of the world's largest atria, at 499 feet (152 m) high. A food court and garage are located in the basement.

Jin Mao Tower contains the world's longest laundry chute, running through the hotel all the way to the basement: almost the full height of the building.

AT+T Corporate Center, 1989, Skidmore, Owings & Merrill Chicago, IL, USA

NBC Tower, 1989, Skidmore, Owings & Merrill Chicago, IL, USA

Trump International Hotel and Tower, 2009, Skidmore, Owings & Merrill Chicago, IL, USA

JIN MAO TOWER
SKIDMORE, OWINGS & MERRILL
1999

Adrian Smith (1944–) was one of the leading designers at Skidmore, Owings & Merrill (SOM) in the 1980s and the leading design partner in the firm's Chicago office in the 1990s. He joined SOM in 1967, while he was finishing his studies at the University of Illinois, and remained there until 2006, when he retired to join in partnership with Canadian-American architect Gordon Gill. While at SOM, Smith became known for his adaptation of historical forms within contemporary high-rises, exemplified by Jin Mao Tower in Shanghai, which recalls traditional Chinese architecture. This can also be seen in Smith's Chicago skyscrapers, such as Olympia Center (1986), with its grand-arched Neiman Marcus store, and the 1920s-style AT+T Corporate Center (1989), as well as the NBC Tower (1989), with its setback limestone facade evoking Raymond Hood's renowned Art Deco RCA Building (1933) in Rockefeller Plaza, New York. Like many other architects in the early 21st century, Smith moved away from overt historical references, such as the iconic pagoda forms seen in Jin Mao Tower, to more modernist designs, notably the Trump International Hotel and Tower (2009) in Chicago and his record-breaking Burj Khalifa in Dubai, which became the world's tallest building when it was completed in 2010.

Within the plans outlined for Pudong in 1993, the Jin Mao Tower was one of several mega high-rises in the commercial district, which sits across the river from the Bund. The Bund district is known for its 1920s European historicist architecture, and Jin Mao reflects that local tradition as well as Smith's facility with creating historicist skyscrapers.

Smith created a pagoda-like high-rise in which the design references the number eight, said in China to be lucky. The eighty-eight-storey building has an octagonal core and its setback heights are determined by mathematical factors of eight, along with eight concrete columns and eight steel ones used to resist typhoon and earthquake damage. The building's address is 88 Century Avenue.

? Businessman Prince Alwaleed bin Talal Abdulaziz Alsaud wanted to build a contemporary urban icon for Riyadh, monolithic and elegant in form, that would be as emblematic as the Eiffel Tower (1889) in Paris, and so the Kingdom Centre was developed. The inverted parabolic top in the upper third of this high-rise was intended to have a dramatic effect on the skyline and has been described as a 'necklace' for the city. It also reflected local planning laws that limited permanent occupancy to the first thirty storeys. A 200-foot-long (60-m) skybridge across the top is used as a public observation deck.

> *Prince Alwaleed wanted a monumental building that he could 'sketch on a napkin'.*
>
> MOHAMMAD AL-ASAD, ARCHITECT

KINGDOM CENTRE
ELLERBE BECKET
2002

Minnesota firm Ellerbe Becket can trace its roots back to 1909, when it was founded by Franklin Ellerbe (1870–1921) and continued by his son, Thomas Ellerbe (1892–1987). The firm practised mostly locally in the Minneapolis-St. Paul area and gained national recognition for the first Mayo Clinic building in 1914. After Thomas's death, the practice merged in 1988 with Los Angeles-based Welton Becket to become Ellerbe Becket. The new firm continued Ellerbe's speciality in health care facilities, such as continued work for the Mayo Clinic and hospitals in Korea and Qatar, and also opened a Kansas City branch that specialized in stadia and sports facilities. The firm grew to some 800 employees in offices across the United States, which garnered regional commissions for corporate high-rises and headquarters, such as the Wells Fargo Tower in Las Vegas (1986). Ellerbe Becket opened offices worldwide in the 1990s from Moscow to Saudi Arabia, the latter winning the Kingdom Centre commission in 1997. The unique Ellerbe Becket design, realized in conjunction with Omrania & Associates, was selected from more than one hundred competition entries. It features a striking inverted catenary arch, which is visible from most parts of Riyadh, becoming a symbol for the city's future in the new millennium.

When it was first constructed, the Kingdom Centre was the tallest building in Saudi Arabia, at 992 feet (302 m). It is currently the second tallest building in the country, the first being the Mecca Royal Clock Tower Hotel (2012) by Dar Al-Handasah, at 1,972 feet (601 m) high. Soon, both will be surpassed by Jeddah's Kingdom Tower, designed in 2011 by Adrian Smith. The Kingdom Tower, when finished in approximately 2019, is intended to be the world's tallest building at 3,281 feet (1,000 m).

Tuntex Sky Tower, 1997,
C.Y. Lee and Hellmuth, Obata and Kassabaum
Kaohsiung, Taiwan

Shanghai World Financial Centre, 2008,
Kohn Pedersen Fox
Shanghai, China

Constructed of steel and reinforced concrete, and clad in reflective glass and aluminium, the complex has fourteen storeys of offices on the lower floors; a luxury Four Seasons hotel; and five storeys of luxury apartments; plus the headquarters of the Kingdom Holding Company on the thirtieth floor. A three-storey shopping centre occupies the granite-clad base.

One floor of the mall is dedicated to women only. Called the Ladies Kingdom, it is staffed by women and contains stores, restaurants and a bank, where women do not have to wear veils.

TORRE MAYOR
ZEIDLER PARTNERSHIP
2003

The fifty-five-storey office tower and retail podium is 738 feet (225 m) high. It was built to withstand earthquakes that measure up to 8.5 on the Richter scale. Torre Mayor contains ninety-six diamond-shaped dampers to absorb these forces and can also resist winds that gust up to 160 miles per hour (257 kph). The building's strength was tested in January 2003 when a 7.6 earthquake shook Mexico City but inflicted no damage to the building. The steel, glass and granite skyscraper has interior finishes of marble and granite. There are twenty-nine lifts that service the building as part of a high-tech building management system, put in place to safeguard occupants.

German-born architect Eberhard Zeidler (1926–) studied in Weimar and Karlsruhe before moving to Canada in 1951. He formed his own firm—Craig, Zeidler and Strong—in 1963 in Toronto and remained there until 1975. He then joined with Alfred C. Roberts to create Zeidler Roberts. The firm executed modern buildings throughout Canada and beyond, including Toronto Eaton Center (1981) and the master plan of Yerba Buena Gardens in San Francisco, executed for Canadian developer Olympia and York (1984), as well as Canada Place (1986) in Vancouver and Place Montréal Trust (1988). The firm specialized in shopping centres and medical facilities but it also produced large commercial high-rises, such as Two Liberty Place (1990) in Philadelphia and Wisma 46 (1996) in Jakarta city centre. When Torre Mayor was designed in 1997, and then built between 1999 and 2003, the team that led its creation were partners Zeidler and Ian Grinnel, along with Dalibor Vokac and Rob Eley, both design architects. Adamson Architects of Toronto were the associates. However, the key to the project's success may well have been Toronto property developer Paul Reichmann, who insisted on a world-class skyscraper that would not only attract high-profile clients to Mexico City but also resist natural disasters.

Wisma 46, 1996,
Zeidler Partnership
Jakarta, Indonesia

Trump International Hotel and Tower, 2012,
Zeidler Partnership
Toronto, Canada

The Bow, 2013,
Zeidler Partnership
Calgary, Canada

When Torre Mayor was topped out in 2002, it surpassed the height of Mexico City's previous record holder—Pemex Executive Tower (1983), designed by Pedro Moctezuma Díaz Infante—by 46 feet (14 m). As with Torre Mayor, Pemex Executive Tower was built to be earthquake resistant and survived a tremor that measured 8.1 in 1985.

Although Zeidler had designed high-rises before, none had been this prominent or this tall. It was a great opportunity for the entire Toronto-based team, because Torre Mayor was to be the most important skyscraper to be built in Mexico City since the earthquake of 1985: a symbol of restored faith. The tower was also intended to help reinvigorate the economy and was conceived principally for offices. However, the two-storey base contains retail and restaurant spaces that the design firm likens to lions' paws reaching out into the plaza. It led Zeidler Partnership to other commissions for taller buildings, from the mixed-use Trump International Hotel and Tower (2012) in Toronto to The Bow (2013) in Calgary with Foster + Partners.

You build on cost and you borrow on value.
PAUL REICHMANN

The amazing thing about this tower is not its height but rather its striking design, a testament to the creativity of Foster in designing an iconic building for London's traditional urban environment without having to make it a behemoth. As with his other buildings, including Commerzbank Headquarters and Hearst Tower, the architect created atria within that are public spaces for the building's occupants.

SWISS RE TOWER
NORMAN FOSTER
2004

The Swiss Re tower, now 30 St. Mary Axe, has become a symbol of 21st-century London, perhaps even more so than the London Eye ferris wheel and Greenwich's Millennium Dome (both 2000). It is the work of Norman Foster (1935–) who is one of England's most prolific architects. Trained at the University of Manchester and Yale University in the early 1960s, he established an architectural practice in London in 1963, partnering with Richard Rogers and others. Foster created his own firm in 1967 and became well known soon afterwards for the sleek Willis Faber & Dumas Headquarters (1975) in Ipswich and the high-tech Hong Kong and Shanghai Bank Headquarters (1986) in Hong Kong. Since then, he has been recognized the world over for his distinctive, mostly steel-and-glass designs, which are not only energy-efficient but also user-friendly, often created with structurally expressive, public garden spaces within. One of the first of these buildings was Commerzbank Headquarters (1997) in Frankfurt. Foster was investigating similar ideas within his ninety-two-storey Millennium Tower in 1996, but its cancellation resulted in a lower-scale opportunity for London. The iconic curvilinear Swiss Re office tower was nicknamed the 'Gherkin' even while it was being designed in 1998 to 1999.

The forty-storey steel-and-glass tower is 590 feet (180 m) high and serviced by twenty-four lifts. On the top floor is a private members' club with panoramic views. The diagonally braced structural skin design, called a 'diagrid', is a fluid one with floors rotated to create voids at the perimeter for atria. The cross-bracing aids wind resistance, and the curved cylindrical shape facilitates wind flow around the building and air circulation within. Double-glazing assists in air circulation during the summer, with passive solar heating in winter.

Commerzbank Headquarters,
1997, **Norman Foster**
Frankfurt, Germany

Hearst Tower, 2006, **Norman Foster** New York, NY, USA

The dynamically curved glazed form has precedents within Foster's earlier work. Examples include Canary Wharf Underground Station (1999) and City Hall (2002), where the bulbous glass facade led to a variety of nicknames, including 'The Onion'. Some have likened its interior to Frank Lloyd Wright's spiral design for the Guggenheim Museum (1959) in New York.

A Roman grave of a teenage girl was unearthed during the pre-construction phase in 1995, and reinserted and rededicated with a memorial marker at the tower's base in 2007.

The concrete fifty-seven-storey tower is 623 feet (190 m) high and contains 147 apartments served by five lifts. The design consists of nine pentagonal segments, five storeys each, that rotate around the core. The lowest two house office spaces.

TURNING TORSO
SANTIAGO CALATRAVA
2005

Spanish-born and Swiss-trained Santiago Calatrava (1951–) is an architect whose structures express movement. After training in Valencia and Zurich, he established his own firm in 1981. Calatrava became known initially for expressively sculptural bridges, such as the Alamillo Bridge (1992) in Seville and the Campo Volantin Footbridge (1997) in Bilbao. The architect also designed sculptural buildings on a larger scale, such as Montjuïc Communications Tower (1992) for the Barcelona Olympic Games and the addition to Milwaukee Art Museum (2001), which incorporates a giant operable sunscreen that is the size of a Boeing 747 airplane wing. The real key to Calatrava's works, however, is art, and he has likened his paintings and sculptures to studies for buildings. This is exemplified in the innovative design of Turning Torso, which recalls *Twisting Torso*, a white marble sculpture by Calatrava.

Like the work of many architects, from Frank Lloyd Wright to Frank Gehry, who have pushed the design limits, Calatrava's oeuvre is not without controversy. The most recent involves the Valencia Opera House (2008), which has received complaints about its peeling paint and poor construction.

I did not want to do stereotypical buildings.

Capital Gate,
2013,
RMJM
Abu Dhabi, UAE

Cayan Tower,
2013,
Skidmore,
Owings & Merrill
Dubai, UAE

The developer of Turning Torso saw Calatrava's *Twisting Torso* sculpture, a series of blocks spiralling around a shaft, and wanted it recreated in a building in Malmo, Sweden. After the tower's success, Calatrava was hired to design the 2,000-foot-high (610 m) Chicago Spire (begun in 2007), which stalled during the economic recession. Other firms have since produced twisting, spiralling skyscrapers in the Middle East.

The metal-panelled building is twelve storeys high and occupies a site of 13,325 square feet (1,238 sq m) on Osaka's main shopping street. The building houses bars, restaurants, a spa and health club, a golf space, and indoor amusements such as video games and *pachinko* machines. Namba Hips promotes its facade as both an hourglass sign denoting eternal time and an exclamation point. However, the entertainment functions within are clearly advertised by a free-fall ride on the facade itself, in which a six-passenger lift is intentionally dropped at breath-taking speed.

Imanishi Motoakasaka, 1991, Shin Takamatsu Tokyo, Japan
Omula Beauty College, 1998, Shin Takamatsu Fukuoka, Japan

The facade features Yabafo, the largest indoor free-fall ride in the world at 242 feet (74 m). In 2011 to 2012 it was partly covered with a rock-climbing wall for a competition.

NAMBA HIPS
SHIN TAKAMATSU
2007

Shin Takamatsu (1948–) has always been an outsider in Japanese architecture, providing individual design statements that are very different from those of his colleagues, whose work is more predictable. Although Takamatsu's vocabulary is usually one of metal, rather than wood or concrete, his building forms are distinctly individual but generally linked by images of industrial and mechanical forms. After studying at Kyoto University, where he specialized in architectural engineering, he established his own design firm in 1980. He soon received acclaim for the overtly machine-age dental clinics Ark (1983) and Pharaoh (1984), as well as the Origin headquarters (1986), all in Kyoto. Quasar (1994), built on Berlin's Frankfurter Allee, attempted to create a commercial landmark for a new Germany that harkened back to the futuristic urban images seen in German movies such as *Metropolis* (1927) and also Berlin's urban environment of the 1920s. The Namba Hips building in Osaka relates to the idea of creating a unique image for an entertainment mall: in some ways a building type that also relates to Japan's sense of compartmentalization and fascination with *pachinko*, or pinball gaming. After reviewing proposals by other architects, the client selected Takamatsu's design because of its proclamation of independence from its surroundings.

Namba Hips draws upon Takamatsu's earlier works in which facades advertise companies. For example, Omula Beauty College (1998) has a giant elongated 'O' for its facade. Geometric forms in which scale is intentionally distorted are Takamatsu's way of making statements stand out in the streetscape.

Takamatsu always creates a distinctive image for clients, and this is no exception. When viewed from the street, the steeply triangular side elevations proclaim that the high-rise is visually different from its rectilinear adjacent buildings. The facade's incised figure-eight form projects its uniqueness when compared with its bland neighbours. In the architect's words, he created a building that is 'polyphonic'.

According to the architects, the design is a square prism that relates to a Chinese symbol for the Earth, intersected by two arcs that suggest the heavens. The void at the top links the two worlds of Heaven and Earth. KPF designed the building in 1993, but it stalled from 1997 to 1998 during the Asian financial crisis. When the project was resurrected, the design increased in height by 104 feet (32 m).

SHANGHAI WORLD FINANCIAL CENTRE
KOHN PEDERSEN FOX
2008

Kohn Pedersen Fox (KPF) is a major U.S. firm known worldwide for its commercial work. It was founded in 1976 by partners A. Eugene Kohn (1930–), William Pedersen (1938–) and Sheldon Fox (1930–2006), with Pedersen essentially in the role of lead designer. All three architects worked in the large office of John Carl Warnecke before establishing KPF. Their sleek, curved-glass 333 Wacker Drive (1983) in Chicago catapulted them to international recognition in skyscraper design, and premium jobs followed in Chicago, Cincinnati, Dallas, Minneapolis, New York and Washington, D.C. Examples range from Procter and Gamble Headquarters (1986) in Cincinnati to the World Bank (1996) in Washington. European jobs paralleled U.S. ones in scale and importance, including Clifford Chance Tower (2002) and KPMG Headquarters (2009), both in Canary Wharf, London, as well as DZ Bank Headquarters (1992) in Frankfurt and Endesa Headquarters (2003) in Madrid. Their work also expanded in Asia and includes JR Central Towers (2000) in Nagoya, Japan, plus a host of buildings in China and the Middle East. Of all these sleek, structurally overt modern buildings, the Shanghai World Financial Centre is perhaps the most striking, bringing to mind the glazed bold form of 333 Wacker Drive, which garnered the firm fame more than twenty-five years earlier.

The 101-storey glass tower is 1,614 feet (492 m) high, and a glass-floored observation deck is at the penultimate level. The base of Brazilian green granite and yellow limestone contains retail space, lower floors have offices, and towards the top is Park Hyatt Hotel. A diagonally braced structural system connected to the building's columns was used within to provide wind bracing. The Council on Tall Buildings and Urban Habitat declared this solution 'nothing short of genius', thus making this gigantic yet elegantly simple form an 'icon of Shanghai and China'.

International Commerce Centre, 2010, KPF
Hong Kong, China

Infinity Tower, 2012, KPF
São Paulo, Brazil

Dramatic voids atop skyscrapers feature on Philip Johnson's AT+T Building (1984) in New York and Ellerbe Becket's Kingdom Centre (2002) in Riyadh. In a way they replace the various skyscraper terminations that were equally dramatic in their time, such as the spire on the Chrysler Building (1929) in New York.

The void was originally circular, a controversial form interpreted as a *Hinomaru* or rising sun. It was redesigned to be rectilinear, which was less expensive to construct.

AQUA TOWER
STUDIO GANG
2010

Aqua is the tallest building in the world created by a female lead designer. It is an eighty-two-storey, 858-foot-high (262 m) multiuse tower and has one of Chicago's largest green roofs. Upper floors contain 476 rental and 263 condominium units, whereas floors one to eighteen house a Radisson Blu hotel. The base contains offices as well as a terrace with gardens and a running track. The metal-and-glass facade encases residential units as expected in any other high-rise building. However, the undulating concrete balconies created with computer-aided design give the building an iconic appearance well beyond any normal apartment building, and function as sunscreens, too.

How do you make a box not look like a box? Chicago architect Jeanne Gang (1964–) provided her solution with Aqua, a residential tower created with architect and developer James R. Loewenberg. Gang graduated from the University of Illinois in 1986 and then studied at ETH in Zurich and at Harvard, earning a master's in architecture at the latter in 1993. She established Studio Gang in 1997, and early works brought her instant acclaim. The Starlight Theater (2003) in Rockford, Illinois, has a movable panelled roof for star-lit evening performances and backlit roundels in its facade that glow at night to represent the cosmos. The Chinese American Service League Kam Liu Center (2004) in Chicago's Chinatown has titanium shingles diagonally placed to project a contemporary image of a dragon's skin, the large glazed second floor of the entrance facade having tones of red and jade green within. Gang's thought-provoking works, including the high-profile Aqua in Chicago, garnered her a MacArthur Foundation fellowship in 2011. More recent commissions include her being part of the team selected to design the interactive Lucas Museum of Narrative Art complex, due to open in 2018, and a hall of residence at the University of Chicago, scheduled for 2016.

Chinese American Service League Kam Liu Center, 2004, Studio Gang
Chicago, IL, USA

Nature Boardwalk, Lincoln Park Zoo, 2010, Studio Gang
Chicago, IL, USA

WMS Boathouse, Clark Park, 2013, Studio Gang
Chicago, IL, USA

Gang often incorporates nature and natural forces within architecture, as seen in the 'Aerospace Design' exhibition (2003) for NASA, in which interwoven curved vitrines displayed historic wind tunnel models, the entirety suggestive of airflow. Her covered boardwalk at Lincoln Park Zoo (2010) was inspired by a turtle's shell, whereas the angled roofs of the WMS Boathouse (2013) project an image of rowers.

Architect and developer Loewenberg brought Gang into this commission to create an apartment tower unlike any other in Chicago. Her dynamic balconies surrounding the rectilinear steel-and-glass apartments at Aqua were inspired by similarly stacked limestone striations around North America's Great Lakes. However, they are also a tangible homage to nature's forces, particularly airflow and water currents.

SOM's contextual design features Islamic decorative detailing in the facade, and the plan is based on the geometric formation of petals of a regional desert flower, the *Hymenocallis*. Influenced by local cultures, the cutting-edge skyscraper was intended to be the centrepiece of a larger city development, and its base contains the Dubai Fountain within a 27-acre (11-ha) park.

BURJ KHALIFA
SKIDMORE, OWINGS & MERRILL
2010

Because of the John Hancock Center (1970) and Sears Tower (1974), both in Chicago, and now Burj Khalifa in Dubai, the firm Skidmore, Owings & Merrill (SOM) has long been associated with the highest of high-rises. Its design archives also include some of the world's tallest buildings that were never constructed, most notably the proposed 2,000-foot (610-m) tower at 7 South Dearborn Street in Chicago (1999). Adrian Smith (1944–) was the design partner on Burj Khalifa: SOM's latest opportunity to create the world's tallest building, far beyond any of its nearest competitors. Working with the team at SOM, particularly structural engineer William Baker, Smith created an architectural and engineering marvel based on the structural tube system that SOM had developed for the Sears and Hancock towers. The architect designed the 2,717-foot (828-m) tower in 2003 and construction began the following year. SOM has a mandatory retirement policy for its partners when they reach the age of sixty-five. In anticipation of this, Smith left in 2006, while the tower was under construction, to start his own firm with Gordon Gill. Together they have continued Smith's work in high-rises by designing what will become the world's tallest tower: the 3,281-foot-high (1,000 m) Kingdom Tower in Saudi Arabia, currently under construction.

I guess the tall building is considered to be my thing.
ADRIAN SMITH

The 163-storey concrete-and-steel multiuse tower is clad in textured aluminium and stainless steel and has an observation deck on the 124th floor. The Y-shaped plan uses a bundled tube system in which walls of tubes buttress one another, with the staggered heights of the tubes acting as structural reinforcement and wind vortex control.

Pearl River Tower, 2011, Adrian Smith + Gordon Gill Architecture
Guangzhou, China

After the destruction of New York's World Trade Center in 2001, pundits questioned whether mega towers would be constructed again. However, humanity's need to surpass previous accomplishments has continued, similar to inter-urban rivalries seven centuries ago, when European cities vied with one another to see who could build the tallest cathedral.

You have made it when your building becomes part of LEGO®'s Landmark Series, which in addition to Burj Khalifa, includes Seattle's Space Needle, the Empire State Building and the Eiffel Tower.

The sixty-eight-storey reflective glass-clad office tower is 861 feet (262.5 m) high. It has a curved heli-pad on the fifty-second floor that cantilevers from the side of the building. The tower is serviced by fourteen lifts. There is an observatory at 597 feet (182 m). The lower six floors house retail and food services, whereas the shaft contains offices, an observation deck—Saigon Skydeck—on the forty-ninth floor, restaurants on floors fifty and fifty-one and a bar on floor fifty-two.

Soldier Field, 2003,
Wood and Zapata
with Lohan Caprile Goettsch
Chicago, IL, USA

Fontainebleau Resort, 2007,
Carlos Zapata
Las Vegas, NV, USA

The Bitexco Financial Tower hosted its first vertical run on 31 October 2011, with German competitor Thomas Dold taking first place with a time of 4 minutes 51 seconds.

BITEXCO FINANCIAL TOWER
CARLOS ZAPATA
2010

Venezuelan-born and New York-based Carlos Zapata (1961–) is not one to publicize himself. Yet his buildings are bold in design, and recently several have achieved international recognition. He has designed modernist luxury homes from Florida to Ecuador. More importantly, he was the lead design talent behind the dramatic yet controversial revamp of Chicago's historic Soldier Field (2003), although he was the least vocal about it among those who were involved. Later work has included glass high-rises such as the unfinished Fontainebleau Resort (2007) in Las Vegas and the planned Turnberry Ocean Club in Sunny Isles, Florida, designed in 2014. He is also responsible for the curvilinear Concourse J with glazed skywalks at Miami International Airport, built in 2006 in conjunction with associates MGE Architects. Despite these successes it was Zapata's design for Bitexco Financial Tower in Ho Chi Minh City, Vietnam, that really catapulted him to international recognition, perhaps well beyond the publicity received for Soldier Field a few years before. Bitexco's chairman, Vu Quang Hoi, intended to make the building a symbol of pride in Vietnam, and Zapata obliged. The tower was built between 2007 and 2010, in conjunction with Jean-Marie Duthilleul and Etienne Tricaud of AREP Group.

Bitexco Financial Tower was the tallest building in Vietnam for a year only, being surpassed in 2012 by the 1,102-foot (336-m) Keangnam Landmark Tower in Hanoi. The latter was designed by a team that included Korean architects Heerim and Samoo, Vietnamese architects Aum & Lee, and U.S. mega firm Hellmuth, Obata and Kassabaum (HOK).

The new building was intended to reflect the aspirations of the Vietnamese people and to become an icon of a newly dynamic nation. Zapata's design team used Vietnam's national flower—the lotus—as inspiration because it is a Vietnamese symbol of purity, optimism and commitment. The striking cantilevered heli-pad also recalls a lotus pad. Bitexco's current chief executive officer, In-Suk Ko, was involved in the initial development of the Bitexco Financial Tower and is heralded for bringing Korean business efficiency to Vietnam.

[In Vietnam] they have a very unique culture of self-criticism. Even their employees' performance evaluations are conducted two-ways rather than top-to-bottom flow.

IN-SUK KO

Capital Gate has a record-breaking lean of 18 degrees, certified by Guinness World Records. By contrast, the legendary Leaning Tower of Pisa (1372) in Italy leans only 3.9 degrees.

Although this masterpiece of construction has influenced other twisted skyscrapers in Shanghai and Dubai, none has Capital Gate's record-breaking lean. The curvaceous building, in which no two floors are the same, relates to the gentle winds and waves, seemingly formed by those natural forces. On one side the glazed sunscreen cape projects the image of a desert traveller. The client—Abu Dhabi National Exhibitions Company—wanted a landmark but futuristic building to celebrate the dynamic role of Abu Dhabi in cutting-edge trade shows. Tony Archibold, then associate director at RMJM Middle East, Dubai, and now design director at Bluehaus, led the team that created this unique design.

**CAPITAL GATE
RMJM
2011**

When Scottish architect Robert Matthew (1906–1975) was apprenticed in his father's architectural practice, Lorrimer & Matthew, and then partnered with Stirrat Johnson-Marshall in 1956, he never dreamed that their venture would become today's mega firm Robert Matthew Johnson-Marshall (RMJM), with more than 1,000 employees in offices spread over the world. Although Robert Matthew had a prominent position as chief architect of the London office in the 1940s, it was during the 1950s and 1960s that RMJM designed modernist classics such as New Zealand House (1963) in London and the Royal Commonwealth Pool (1970) in Edinburgh. However, its work for the Scottish Parliament (2004) in Edinburgh, designed by Catalan architect Enric Miralles with RMJM as associate architects, was controversial because of schedule delays and cost overruns. After a reorganization in 2009 and continued expansion through the acquisition of other companies, RMJM's international reach now includes more than a dozen built high-rises, such as the 636-foot (208-m) Seba Tower (2011) in Abu Dhabi and the 682-foot (208-m) China Merchants Bank Tower (2013) in Shanghai. What helped put RMJM on the international map was Capital Gate, also known as the Leaning Tower of Abu Dhabi, begun in 2007.

This tour-de-force high-rise served as a challenge to other firms. Consequently, twisting, gyrating towers can be seen today in Shanghai and Dubai, and others are on the electronic drawing board, such as Studio Gang's San Francisco high-rise. However, Frank Gehry had already created a smaller precedent in his Dancing House (1996) in Prague.

It takes forty days to clean the hotel exterior with a team of approximately ten people.

**VANDANA KUMARI,
HOUSEKEEPING MANAGER**

The 540-foot (165-m) tower has a pre-cambered concrete core, with varying floor plates enclosed by a diagrid steel structure, clad in steel and glass. The tornado-like shape widens at the top to accommodate the Hyatt Hotel with a central atrium and 189 rooms between floors eight and thirty-three. The site's extreme temperature variations impacted on the steel structure's expansion and contraction, making it a challenge to glaze. Each of the 12,500 triangular glass panes is different.

Infinity Tower, 2013, Skidmore, Owings & Merrill
Dubai, UAE

Shanghai Tower, 2015, Gensler
Shanghai, China

OMA has created a number of new skyscraper designs across Asia and Europe. The first was the Rothschild Bank Headquarters (2011) in London and the most recent is De Rotterdam (2014). All the high-rises within this period are characterized by glazed, blocky, rectilinear forms that are often offset.

**CCTV HEADQUARTERS
REM KOOLHAAS
2012**

Rotterdam-born Rem Koolhaas (1944–) has always pushed intellectual and actual boundaries in architecture, a trait that helped garner him the Pritzker Architecture Prize in 2000. After studying at the Architectural Association in London, he travelled to the United States on a fellowship. It was during this period that he wrote his landmark book *Delirious New York* (1978). This was followed by the philosophical *S, M, L, XL* (1995), and both became classics within the architectural community. Koolhaas was one of the founders of the Office for Metropolitan Architecture (OMA) in 1975. The firm built structures such as the Netherlands Dance Theatre (1987), The Hague, considered one of the major buildings of the era. International commissions followed, including McCormick Tribune Campus Center at Illinois Institute of Technology (2003) and Seattle Public Library (2004). Koolhaas consistently shed historic references in favour of creative space planning and new interpretations of modernist vocabulary, exemplified by his CCTV Headquarters in Beijing. Its design paved the way for even larger commercial buildings.

Shenzhen Stock Exchange, 2013, Rem Koolhaas
Shenzhen, China

The Interlace, 2013, Rem Koolhaas
Singapore

Koolhaas's fifty-four-storey building features a rectilinear loop of six steel-and-glass diagrid sections. The complex is 768 feet (234 m) high with a 246-foot (75-m) cantilever. Serviced by seventy-five lifts, the two towers contain offices: editorial in one and news broadcasting in the other, while the cantilevered bridge houses administrative functions. In contrast to the building's orthogonal forms, there is a circular steel heli-pad on its top.

Koolhaas planned to break the mould in skyscraper design with the distinctively shaped headquarters for China Central TV. Instead of creating a vertical flat mass more typical of skyscrapers, his design disassembled and then reassembled rectilinear parts into an interconnected monumental form, becoming a giant three-dimensional sculptural experience visible throughout the city.

Because of its distinctive shape locals have nicknamed the building 'big pants' or 'big boxer shorts'. During construction it had been billed as 'China's answer to the Arc de Triomphe'.

Standing 1,016 feet (309 m) high, the steel-and-glass building has eight double-skinned, naturally ventilated facades. The extra white glass reflects the ever-changing sky. Above the lobby is a retail space; the lower floors house offices, the middle section contains a hotel, and at the top are apartments and a viewing deck.

THE SHARD
RENZO PIANO
2012

Italian architect Renzo Piano (1937–) is known for museum design. Buildings such as the Menil Collection (1986) in Houston and Morgan Library (2006) in New York generally project a restrained elegant modernism, often with skeletal detailing. After graduating from the Polytechnic University of Milan in 1964, he worked within his father's construction company and with several architects, including Louis Kahn, before establishing the Renzo Piano Building Workshop. Piano is above all a builder and produces beautiful buildings both tiny and mega scale. Larger constructions range from the San Nicola Football Stadium (1990) in Bari, Italy, to Kansai International Airport Terminal (1994), near Osaka. These earned him numerous awards, including the Pritzker Architecture Prize in 1998. He added high-rise commercial structures to his oeuvre in the 1990s, such as the twenty-two-storey Debis Tower (1998) in Berlin and the forty-one-storey Aurora Place (2000) in Sydney. These were topped by the fifty-two-storey New York Times Building (2007). All paved the way for The Shard, officially the London Bridge Tower, built with Adamson Associates.

Aurora Place,
2000,
Renzo Piano
Sydney, Australia

New York Times Building, 2007,
Renzo Piano
New York,
NY, USA

Obelisk-shaped mega tower designs were prepared by Denton Corker Marshall and Harry Seidler & Associates in the late 1990s for Melbourne's Grollo Tower. Neither came to fruition because of financing. Piano's creation of The Shard as a slender pyramid, with its termination open, seems to have influenced a similar design by KPF for Lotte World Tower (estimated 2016) in Seoul.

> The spire concept
> . . . it belongs to our
> imaginations. It's also
> about—and this may
> be a bit poetic—
> breathing fresh air.

Piano's intention was to build a 'vertical town'. He suggested a tapering spire not only to differentiate between the various functions—from commercial to offices to residential—but also so that the building 'disappeared into the clouds'. Constructed at the site of a transit hub next to London Bridge Station, The Shard has become a symbol of urban regeneration and an icon within London's skyline. When it was completed, the £430 million tower became the tallest building in Europe.

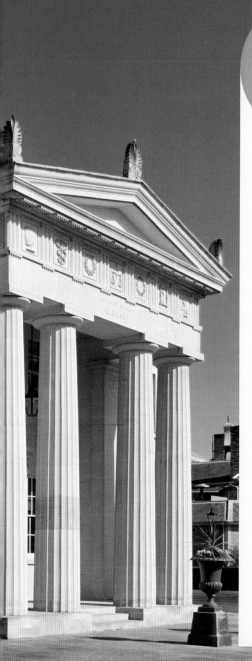

CHAPTER FIVE
HOMAGE TO THE PAST

This chapter focuses on the power of the past to captivate us, no matter how contemporary we may think we are. Whether overtly historicist—Lev Rudnev in the 1950s and Quinlan Terry in the 1990s—or more sophisticated in the use of iconic historic imagery—Rafael Moneo, Helmut Jahn and Kisho Kurokawa in the 1980s—buildings in this chapter demonstrate the persistence of the past within contemporary society. This includes the clever reuse of historic structures by Diller, Scofidio and Renfro in New York and by Nicholas Grimshaw in Mexico. Beyond history, local context and building traditions also provide inspiration, as seen in works by Glenn Murcutt and Kengo Kuma.

❮ Maitland Robinson Library, Cambridge, UK

Stalin built seven high-rises, instead of completing the Palace of the Soviets mega tower, because Moscow had no skyscrapers and therefore did not compare with other cities, particularly capitalist ones. Sites were selected in 1947, and Stalin chose the architects in 1947 and 1948. Rudnev, a rising star in the communist party, received the plum job for the tallest building, the university.

Even before cosmonaut training was instituted in 1960, lifts at Moscow State University were used by volunteers in free-falling weightless experiments, the fall being cushioned by air brakes.

Rudnev also designed the comparable Palace of Culture and Science (1955) in Warsaw, planned as a university but utilized as offices. The building's height, with spire, is 778 feet (237 m), appropriately deferential to Moscow's university. Rudnev modelled some of its decorative detailing on historic palaces and villas in Poland.

MOSCOW STATE UNIVERSITY
LEV RUDNEV
1954

The death of Joseph Stalin in 1953 and the subsequent rise of Nikita Khrushchev impacted on Soviet architecture. Almost overnight, unnecessary architectural ornament was outlawed. However, Moscow State University, designed by Lev Rudnev (1885–1956), is one of the so-called wedding cake 'Seven Sisters' skyscrapers in Moscow, commissioned by Stalin in 1948. Rudnev attended the Imperial Academy of Arts in St. Petersburg and graduated in 1915. After the socialist revolution in 1917, he won the competition to build the simple red granite Monument to the Fallen Fighters (1919) in St. Petersburg. With Stalin's rise in the 1930s, the architect was awarded high-profile commissions such as Frunze Military Academy (1937) in Moscow, a classically detailed building with a bold, gridded, block-like facade, intended to project the strength of the Red Army. Rudnev's post-World War II work included the reconstruction of destroyed cities and public buildings from Warsaw to Baku. It is perhaps fortunate that Rudnev did not live to see the changes that may have led to his 're-education' by the Party.

Government House, 1952, Lev Rudnev
Baku, Azerbaijan

Palace of Culture and Science, 1955, Lev Rudnev
Warsaw, Poland

The thirty-nine-storey structure is 784 feet (239 m) high and was supposedly the world's tallest building outside of New York until 1969. The steel frame has masonry and concrete infill and sits atop an enormous concrete foundation. Exterior masonry and terracotta tiles were affixed to the frame with stainless-steel anchors. The construction of this and six other towers diverted resources from creating housing. Khrushchev changed this after Stalin's death.

Berlin's Kaiser Wilhelm Memorial Church (1963) is similar to Coventry Cathedral. Architect Egon Eiermann incorporated the ruins of its Romanesque bell tower into his new church as a symbol of reconstruction. It has a cross of nails from the original roof of Coventry Cathedral as a symbol of reconciliation.

COVENTRY CATHEDRAL

BASIL SPENCE

1962

Throughout World War II, European cities experienced mass destruction. Reconstruction afterwards sometimes combined modernist aesthetics with historicist forms and historic ruins. One such example is Coventry Cathedral by Basil Spence (1907–1976), constructed adjacent to the ruins of the medieval St. Michael's Cathedral, severely damaged in the German bombing of 14 November 1940. Born in India, Spence studied in Edinburgh from 1919 to 1925, then served an apprenticeship with Sir Edwin Lutyens, one of Britain's great architects. Spence started a practice with William Kininmonth in 1931 during the Great Depression. It later merged with Rowand Anderson and Paul, with whom Spence designed pavilions for Glasgow's Empire Exhibition (1938). After service in the British army as a camouflage officer, Spence returned postwar to work briefly in the Rowand office before setting up his own firm. He made an early mark on British modern architecture with exhibition design, particularly the Sea and Ships Pavilion at the Festival of Britain (1951). His big break, however, came when he was selected for the new Coventry Cathedral in 1951. This important commission led to further high-profile works, including Glasgow's airport (1966), the British Pavilion for Expo '67 in Montreal (1967) and the British Embassy in Rome (1968).

The red sandstone walls match the tone of the old cathedral. The new 79-foot (24-m) manganese bronze alloy spire, topped with a 12-foot (3.6-m) aluminium sculpture of a winged cross designed by Geoffrey Clarke, was brought in by helicopter and put in place in 1962.

Spence's design was selected in 1951 from 200 competition entries. In the church the architect used masonry modern forms with historic references to Gothic ribs within the vaulted interiors. He purposely left the ruined 14th-century cathedral as part of his plan: a symbol of healing and resurrection. He also worked with prominent artists, including sculptor Jacob Epstein, who created the *St. Michael and the Devil* (1956–1958) entrance sculpture. Spence was knighted in 1960 for his design, before the building was finished.

The Royal Mint supplied more than fifty newly minted pennies to be set within the cathedral floor to mark a processional path for the clergy.

Kaiser Wilhelm Memorial Church, 1963,
Egon Eiermann
Berlin, Germany

The fountain is surrounded by concentric colonnades designed as a pastiche of Roman and Renaissance forms, creatively using water sprays, neon lights and stainless steel to bring these details up to the 1970s and 1980s. The dominant materials are granite, marble, stucco and stainless steel. A restoration carried out in 2004 by the adjacent Loews Hotel helped to retain the plaza's original impact, despite the elimination of a campanile.

In collaboration with Perez Associates, Moore created Piazza d'Italia not only as a monument to New Orleans's Italian-American community, but also as a neighbourhood development anchor in the city's Warehouse District. He provided a fountain and a plaza that reinterpreted—in design expression and contemporary, theatrical detail—Italian classical forms for the hip postmodern era. The fountain's plan was based on the map of Italy. New Orleans's mayor Moon Landrieu enlisted Moore to design the fountain and the plaza as part of a plan to improve the city's economy.

*Kresge College, University
of California,* 1971,
Charles Moore
Santa Cruz, CA, USA

*Haas School of Business,
University of California,*
1995, Charles Moore
Berkeley, CA, USA

PIAZZA D'ITALIA
CHARLES MOORE
1978

When Piazza d'Italia in New Orleans was unveiled, it became a sensation: an instant icon of postmodern classicism for the next decade. Although its architect, Charles Moore (1925–1993), had already achieved professional recognition for the shingle-style modernist Sea Ranch (1963), California, the Piazza d'Italia catapulted him to international 'starchitect' status. Born in Benton Harbor, Michigan, Moore graduated from the University of Michigan in 1947 and continued his studies at Princeton until 1957. He worked as a teaching assistant for Louis Kahn and afterwards entered into a lifetime of academic practice. This included long-term teaching stints at University of California, Berkeley; Yale School of Architecture; University of California, Los Angeles; and University of Texas at Austin, to which he left his important archive. In 1997, his estate established a foundation within the city, based at his former home and studio, which supports architectural programmes and residencies for young architects from abroad. Throughout his influential academic career, Moore also practised architecture with various partners. This was usually in an architectural co-operative, one of which was Moore Ruble Yudell, established in 1977 with John Ruble and Buzz Yudell and still in existence today. Moore designed mostly buildings for universities, from California to Taiwan, but of all his projects, the urban public square in New Orleans was the most important and perhaps the most neglected.

A portrait of Moore is sculpted within two roundels that flank one of the arches, each spraying water into the central fountain.

Although it took several decades to achieve, the Warehouse District in New Orleans is now a neighbourhood with an active gallery scene. It also has an important institutional anchor in the National World War II Museum, which opened in 2000 as part of a master plan developed by Voorsanger Architects from New York.

ANTIGONE HOUSING
RICARDO BOFILL
1980s

Barcelona-born Ricardo Bofill (1939–) was brought up in a construction family and studied architecture in his native city and also in Geneva. He returned home in 1963, and established his well-known firm, Taller de Arquitectura.

Bofill's early works have a visible relationship to regional architectural traditions and are inventive, boldly scaled compositions. Examples include the stacked housing known as Xanadu (1971), which was an experiment in making a multifamily garden tower of summer homes within one structure, and the nearby Muralla Roja (1973) in Calpe, in which the red-toned walls refer to the city construction of Mediterranean Arab architecture. Around this time Bofill left Spain for work in France, developing monumental architectural forms that related to French cultural traditions. The best-known examples of these designs can be seen in several housing projects of the late 1970s. One of these is Antigone in Montpellier, a grand scheme typical of big-picture planning and architecture of the French Grand Projets in the 1980s. Unlike those individual large buildings, Bofill's classical apartment blocks in Antigone were built on a massive urban scale that provided hundreds, and at times thousands, of residential units. Their prominence in subsequent years led to an expansion of Bofill's work around the globe, from the classically inspired Swift Headquarters (1989) in Belgium to sleek glass forms without any classical references, such as Terminal 2 at Barcelona Airport and the W Barcelona Hotel (both 2009).

Les Arcades du Lac, 1982, Ricardo Bofill
Saint-Quentin-en-Yvelines, France

Les Echelles du Baroque, 1985, Ricardo Bofill
Paris, France

 Bofill designed other classically detailed masonry structures throughout the 1980s and 1990s, although perhaps not as exuberant as Antigone. These include masonry and glass skyscrapers such as the United Building (1992) and Citadel Center (2003), both in Chicago.

 In the Greek tragedy, Antigone is a heroine who dies because she believes in divine law above human edicts.

The massive site is 89 acres (36 ha). This mini city includes several buildings that incorporate more than 4,000 residential units in seven-storey blocks, plus 215,000 square feet (20,000 sq m) of commercial space. The buildings are precast concrete.

[I call it] Versailles for the people.

Mayor of Montpellier Georges Frêche wanted to expand the city between the River Lez and the historic core. Bofill provided a master plan that was articulated with uniformly styled classical buildings that drew on the traditions of like-styled squares, plazas and crescents of 18th-century European cities. Large-scale, classically detailed housing projects such as Antigone earned Bofill the appellation 'father of European postmodernism' and led to housing commissions in and around Paris.

The three-storey dental clinic, comprising 1,646 square feet (153 sq m), is built of steel and concrete. The exterior has a single row of smokestack-like lanterns, and the giant industrial fitting attached to the facade resembles the front of a steam locomotive engine.

ARK

SHIN TAKAMATSU

1983

Modernists during the 1920s and 1930s championed an aesthetic appreciation of machines, and pundits often cited one of the pioneers of modern architecture, Le Corbusier: 'A house is a machine in which to live.' Yet Le Corbusier's love of machinery recalls the Industrial Revolution of the 19th century, from the engineering triumphs of Gustave Eiffel and Isambard Kingdom Brunel to architectural design terms such as 'Steamboat Gothic', used to describe Gothic-style buildings along the Ohio and Mississippi River valleys. Design fascination with machines, particularly transport machinery such as airplanes and trains, permeated architecture, informing early buildings by Japanese architect Shin Takamatsu (1948–), for example. Two of Takamatsu's designs that demonstrate his obsession with engineering and machine imagery are dental clinics—the Ark (1983) and Pharaoh (1984)—both in Kyoto, Japan. They are representational, comparable to the way in which Western postmodernists designed buildings that referenced historic stylistic solutions, although these were often classical as opposed to industrial.

The Ark has been called a postmodern folly, although the term 'architectural folly' in the traditional sense might be more appropriately applied to Charles Moore's classical Piazza d'Italia (1978) in New Orleans. The Ark does not invoke classical precedents, yet its focus on large-scale industrial form bears comparison with mega scale in works by Terry Farrell and the fascination with industrial detailing by Nicholas Grimshaw.

 Oxford Ice Rink, 1984, Nicholas Grimshaw Oxford, UK

MI6, 1994, Terry Farrell London, UK

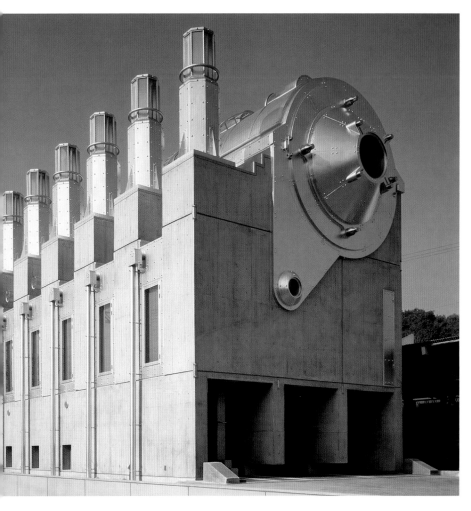

Takamatsu's background in engineering informed his decision to utilize machine imagery in the Ark. The design harkens back directly to the early 19th-century forms of the Industrial Revolution, particularly imagery related to power, torque, speed and acceleration. These characteristics are best exemplified by steam locomotives of that era, but can also be observed in any number of large power plants, which Takamatsu says he drew upon subconsciously as he sketched out the building's design. The site adjacent to a mass transit railway station also reinforces this historic transport association.

With open offices surrounding it and retail services at the lower levels, the central atrium was intended to relate to centrally planned, domical, state capitol buildings, and also to symbolize the openness of government. The atrium within this building was a starting point for the architect's later spaces, particularly the Sony Center (2000) in Berlin. Illinois governor James R. Thompson chose Jahn to design the building.

Munich Airport Centre, Franz Josef Strauss International Airport, 1999, Helmut Jahn
Munich, Germany

STATE OF ILLINOIS CENTER
HELMUT JAHN
1985

Government buildings can be controversial, especially when taxpayers' money is used to construct them. The State of Illinois Center (renamed the James R. Thompson Center in 1993, after the state governor who commissioned it) is no exception. Its controversies ranged from using South African steel at a time when the region's steel mills were closing, to heating and cooling problems in the completely glazed workplace, and also computer operators not being able to see their screens because of the glare. However, with the problems and nicknames put aside—it has been called Chicago's Eyeful Tower, Starship Chicago, Taj Mahal and Thompson's Folly, among the milder appellations—German-American architect Helmut Jahn (1940–) of Murphy/Jahn gave the city a memorable architectural image of government. Born in Nuremberg, Jahn graduated from the Technische Hochschule in Munich in 1965 and arrived in Chicago the following year. He worked with Gene Summers at C.F. Murphy Associates from 1967 and became the firm's executive vice president and director of design in 1973. One of his first major commissions was the Kemper Arena (1974) in Kansas City. Its roof collapse during a storm in 1979 was a learning experience for both engineers and architects, enabling Jahn to continue to create large open spaces within his tech-orientated vocabulary.

The steel-and-glass curved building cost $173 million to realize. It has sky blue, red and salmon-coloured glazing at the lower levels and throughout the interior, which harkens back to 1950s car design. The building sits on a city block, with a Stonehenge-like polychrome masonry wall defining the site line of the 1920s Sherman Hotel that previously stood here, its convex glazed plaza entrance facing the granite memory. The central atrium is seventeen storeys and 308 feet (94 m) high and 160 feet (49 m) in diameter. It is accessed by freestanding lifts and cantilevered staircases. The ground floor, where the food court is located, has a marble and granite pattern akin to those seen in earlier domed government buildings.

Jahn's 1980s buildings are steel-and-glass modernist in vocabulary and Art Deco in overall image, such as the Chicago Board of Trade Building addition (1980) and Northwestern Atrium Center (1987), also in Chicago. Since then his style has been clean-lined and includes larger spaces in Munich, Berlin and Bangkok.

Jahn has been branded with nicknames such as 'Baron von High Tech', 'Genghis Jahn' and 'Flash Gordon' for his 1980s buildings, including the State of Illinois Center.

Two brick arched buildings flank a Roman road and are the gallery and administrative sides of the complex. The museum display building is three storeys high atop a crypt. Skylights provide natural illumination for the main exhibition space, which has transverse arches that define ten bays within. Moneo designed the artefact installations as well as the building.

NATIONAL MUSEUM OF ROMAN ART
RAFAEL MONEO
1986

Spanish architect Rafael Moneo (1937–) earned his architectural degree from Madrid University in 1961. He moved briefly to Denmark to be apprenticed to Jørn Utzon, designer of Sydney's Opera House, whom he admired for his simple monumental designs within the 'heroic' period of modern architecture. Moneo returned to Spain in 1962 and won a competition to design space within the Spanish Academy in Rome. He began teaching in Spain in 1965 and then started his own practice: his first important commissions included the simple, blocky Diestre Factory (1967) in Zaragoza and the massive balconied Urumea Residential Building (1972) in San Sebastián. However, the job that elevated his career to the next level, internationally, was Bankinter (1976) in Madrid, a simple brick office building in which the fenestration recalls Italian architect Aldo Rossi's work of the time. Moneo's simple but strong design for the National Museum of Roman Art in Mérida, Spain, raised his profile further, leading to major commissions such as Madrid's Atocha Railway Station (1992) and the Audrey Jones Beck Building (2000) at the Museum of Fine Arts in Houston, Texas. All Moneo's buildings are characterized by simple geometric massing, usually in masonry. He was awarded the Pritzker Architecture Prize in 1996.

The city of Mérida is known for its Roman ruins, so Moneo's arched building is designed to be compatible with the archaeological finds, perhaps even more so than the glazed wing built for the Egyptian Temple of Dendur in New York.

? The impetus to build the National Museum of Roman Art dates back to 1975 and coincided with Mérida's celebrations of its bimillennium. Archaeological excavations of the site had revealed Roman ruins, such as domestic dwellings, a necropolis, a section of road and part of an aqueduct, and a key component of Moneo's design was the preservation in situ of these archaeological remains. Moneo was selected in 1979, and construction began in 1981.

Getty Villa, 1974,
Robert Langdon
and David Wilson
Santa Monica, CA, USA

*Temple of Dendur
Installation, Metropolitan
Museum of Art*, 1978,
Roche-Dinkeloo
New York, NY, USA

Although El-Wakil is best known for his mosques in the 1980s, especially in Saudi Arabia during its oil-supported building boom, he has practised and taught architecture in both Miami and London. One of his more important institutional buildings is the Oxford Centre for Islamic Studies (2014), which includes a mosque with a minaret.

Mahmoud Bodo Rasch, designer of the Quba Mosque's movable sunscreen roof, was a student of Frei Otto in Stuttgart. Rasch created retractable sunshade umbrellas for several sites in Saudi Arabia, including the Prophet's Holy Mosque (2009) in Medina.

Suleiman Mosque, 1980, Abdel-Wahed El-Wakil
Jeddah, Saudi Arabia

Harithy Mosque, 1986, Abdel-Wahed El-Wakil
Jeddah, Saudi Arabia

Qiblatain Mosque, 1989, Abdel-Wahed El-Wakil
Medina, Saudi Arabia

QUBA MOSQUE RECONSTRUCTION
ABDEL-WAHED EL-WAKIL
1987

Cairo-born Abdel-Wahed El-Wakil (1943–) has made his mark in designing mosques using traditional materials: buildings that accommodate the liturgical requirements and expectations of contemporary worshippers. His historically designed buildings garnered him several awards including the Aga Khan Award for Architecture (1980 and 1989) and the Driehaus Architecture Prize (2009) for traditional buildings. After graduating in 1965 he served an apprenticeship with Hassan Fathy, who became a role model in reconciling modern needs with traditional building methods of Egyptian architecture. El-Wakil taught architecture in the 1960s and 1970s and began his own architectural practice in 1972, designing traditional Egyptian houses. He soon expanded his residential design practice into Saudi Arabia and Kuwait, creating large-scale villas such as Al-Sulaiman Palace (1984) in Jeddah. Awareness of this important house led to more work, including the fifteen mosques he built during the 1980s. Of these, perhaps the most important is the Quba Mosque in Medina. It is built on the site of the first mosque in Islam (622), the construction of which was begun by the Prophet Muhammad and altered several times through the 19th century.

The new mosque's prayer hall accommodates 20,000 worshippers, including 7,000 women. It connects to ablution rooms, residential space, offices and a library. Four minarets and multiple domes mark the prayer hall. The courtyard is built of black, red and white marble and is screened by a movable PVC foam polyester roof.

? El-Wakil's Quba Mosque on the outskirts of the city was part of a larger building campaign organized by the Saudi Ministry of Pilgrimage and Endowment. The architect intended to incorporate portions of the original structure within his design, but this proved impossible because the building needed to accommodate an ever expanding number of worshippers. Instead, he created a new building that harkens back to Medina's minimalist, simple design traditions yet incorporates air conditioning and movable sunshading.

"

To abandon tradition, to disregard the achievements and models of the past and to be caught up in the trauma of change means to be incapable of handling the new.

? This was a particularly daring design in Vienna, a city steeped in architectural tradition by early modern heroes such as Josef Hoffmann, Adolf Loos and Otto Wagner. If the commission had been given to any one of Coop Himmelb(l)au's Viennese contemporaries, there would have been a contextually classical addition instead of this dynamic steel-and-glass concoction. The firm's design individualism was, in some ways, more akin to that of architects working in Graz, such as Günther Domenig.

LAW OFFICE ADDITION
COOP HIMMELB(L)AU
1988

Is it a bird, is it a plane, is it Coop Himmelb(l)au? The seemingly haphazard addition that appears atop a traditional masonry building became an icon of the Deconstructivist movement of the late 1980s and 1990s, with its active disregard for postmodern contextualism and classicism, and its re-imagination of the classic modernist vocabulary of steel and glass. Wolf D. Prix (1942–) and Helmut Swiczinsky (1944–) founded the Viennese firm Coop Himmelb(l)au in 1968. Early on, within their manifesto *Architecture Must Blaze* (1980), they espoused radical principles: that architecture must be dramatically reconfigured. This law office addition in Vienna and the addition to the Funder Factory in St. Veit (1988) pushed the firm to the foreground and garnered international recognition. That recognition led to the firm opening a Los Angeles office, and designing exhibitions and buildings in the United States and Europe. In the United States, these range from the 'Expressionist Utopias' installation at the Los Angeles County Museum of Art (1993) to the Akron Art Museum addition (2007). In Europe, notable buildings include the SEG Apartment Tower (1995) in Vienna, UFA Cinema Centre (1998) in Dresden and BMW Welt (2007) in Munich.

The programme called for a conference room and office addition atop the existing building in Falkestrasse. Coop Himmelb(l)au denies that its design has anything to do with a bird perched on a building, citing instead a lightning bolt. The taut steel arc acts as a spine for the project. Constructed in 1987 to 1988, the steel-and-glass two-storey addition encompasses 4,305 square feet (400 sq m). It incorporates a sizable conference area of 969 square feet (90 sq m).

Adler Planetarium Sky Pavilion, 1998, Lohan Associates
Chicago, IL, USA

Center of Science and Industry, 1999, Arata Isozaki
Columbus, OH, USA

Modern additions to older buildings are rarely as radically conceived as Coop Himmelb(l)au's. The Adler Planetarium (1998) in Chicago was designed by Lohan Associates as a glass-and-concrete addition, which predictably parallels the forms and wall planes of historic buildings, though in a simpler geometric expression. This is very different from the intentional visual irrationality of Coop Himmelb(l)au's addition.

We want architecture that has more. Architecture that bleeds, that exhausts, that whirls, and even breaks.

? Situated atop Hijiyama mountain, Hiroshima City Museum of Contemporary Art overlooks the city destroyed by the atomic bomb on 6 August 1945. As part of his philosophy of symbiosis, the architect combined Asian and Western historic and site-specific elements within his design, and the museum's trademark rotunda recalls the traditionally domed art museums from the early 1900s, except here the circular form is broken or notched to indicate the view towards the city. Kurokawa's passion for museums began with his National Museum of Ethnology (1977) in Osaka.

In all, the steel and reinforced concrete art museum comprises a total of 24,572 square feet (2,282 sq m). Its open-air central space functions as a meeting point for gallery wings that extend longitudinally, their gabled roofs intended to project the image of a village. The stones in the plaza that surrounds the supporting columns of the broken metal-panelled rotunda were salvaged from the bomb-damaged ruins of the city below.

Architecture is a spiritual statement and an expression of thought of the age in which it is created.

*Museum of
Modern Art*, 1994,
Kisho Kurokawa
Wakayama, Japan

*Fukui Prefectural Dinosaur
Museum*, 2000,
Kisho Kurokawa
Fukui, Japan

**HIROSHIMA
CITY MUSEUM OF
CONTEMPORARY ART
KISHO KUROKAWA
1989**

Born into a family of architects, Kisho Kurokawa (1934–2007) will be remembered for being one of the leaders of Japan's Metabolist movement in architecture during the 1960s. Two buildings in particular— Nakagin Capsule Tower (1972) in Tokyo and Sony Tower (1976) in Osaka—are tangible reminders of his importance in shaping ideas whereby cities and buildings can grow organically in a modular way using mass-produced architectural elements. Yet his career was much richer than these constructions alone. Kurokawa was one of Japan's intellectual architectural forces, graduating from Kyoto University in 1957 and studying for advanced degrees from the University of Tokyo. He espoused a symbiotic relationship between modern, Western and Asian forms within his buildings, and began his prolific architecture practice in 1962. Examples of his award-winning work can be seen throughout Japan as well as in Europe, the United States and Asia. They range from Osaka Prefectural Government Offices (1988) to the Sporting Club (1990) in Chicago, Kuala Lumpur International Airport (1998) and the Van Gogh Museum addition (1998) in Amsterdam. It was in the field of museums and cultural buildings that Kurokawa really made his mark, building fourteen throughout his career.

Architect of the Hiroshima Peace Memorial Museum (1955) Kenzo Tange influenced a number of architects, including Kurokawa who was supervised by Tange at the University of Tokyo.

The Hiroshima museum symbolizes not only recognition of the past but also hope for society's future because of the contemporary art displayed within. Its design links the building to the skeletal dome of the 1945 ruins below in the city's Peace Memorial Park. It is comparable with Basil Spence's Coventry Cathedral (1962) and Egon Eiermann's Kaiser Wilhelm Memorial Church in Berlin (1963), acknowledging horrors of a wartime past but also looking beyond to a new postwar era.

Similar to 18th- and 19th-century buildings that incorporated design details from Greco-Roman antiquities, Maitland Robinson Library's south facade has a portico modelled on the Doric Portico of Augustus in Athens. The lantern atop is reminiscent of the marble Roman Tower of the Winds, also in Athens. The interior features a grand staircase that is Georgian in style. The library's 50,000 volumes are accessible to University of Cambridge students and faculty.

MAITLAND ROBINSON LIBRARY
QUINLAN TERRY
1993

Quinlan Terry (1937–) is not alone as a practitioner of traditionally styled architecture in the 20th and 21st centuries. There is a number of architects and clients within architecture today who espouse a return to traditional building forms and construction methods, anachronistic as they may seem. The buildings are sometimes labelled under the heading New Classicism, and Terry's work, mostly in England, represents but one voice in this conservative choir. Born in London, Terry was educated at the Architectural Association in the 1960s and began work in 1962 with classicist Raymond Erith, later becoming a partner in Erith & Terry until 2004. He now works in partnership with his son in the firm of Quinlan and Francis Terry Architects. Terry's earlier works were considered Palladian in inspiration, including Waverton House (1980) in Gloucestershire and Newfield Park (1981) in Yorkshire. Soon his projects grew in scale to include commercial and institutional buildings, such as Richmond's Riverside Development (1988) and the Greek Revival Maitland Robinson Library of Downing College, Cambridge. Terry has received numerous awards for his highly detailed work, including the Richard H. Driehaus Prize in 2005.

Terry was employed by Margaret Thatcher to refurbish the interior of 10 Downing Street. He is said to be Prince Charles's favourite architect.

Let us use the Doric, Ionic and Corinthian orders . . . so that our buildings will be signs and heralds of a more natural, more stable and more beautiful world.

New Classicism has devotees across the globe and architect and theorist Léon Krier, whose retro-inspired works and ideas were widely published in the 1980s, is arguably its guru. Investment manager Richard Driehaus recognized these traditional efforts when he established the Richard H. Driehaus Prize at the University of Notre Dame in Indiana, the first of which was awarded to Krier in 2003.

Downing College is a classically designed complex founded in 1800 and as such is one of the newest colleges at Cambridge. Greek Revivalist William Wilkins created the master plan but reduced endowment supported only part of the massive masonry construction, and the remainder or third side of the court was built in 1951. Terry had made several like-styled masonry additions to the college before this library. The Butterfield building dates to the late 1980s, and more recently the Howard Theatre (2010) was designed with his son Francis.

Vitruvian House, 1990, Thomas Gordon Smith South Bend, IN, USA

Place de Toscane, 2006, Pier Carlo Bontempi Val d'Europe, France

MARIKA-ALDERTON HOUSE
GLENN MURCUTT
1994

Glenn Murcutt (1936–), born in England and raised in New Guinea and Australia, is a master when it comes to combining a minimalist modernist aesthetic with vernacular traditions. There are few who can do this so well. Murcutt was influenced by the minimalism of Ludwig Mies van der Rohe, and similar homes by Richard Neutra and Craig Ellwood. Beyond them, he appreciated native constructions in New Guinea. Murcutt graduated from Sydney Technical College with a diploma in architecture in 1961. After travelling he began work in Sydney in 1964 with the firm Ancher, Mortlock, Murray and Woolley, and then started his own practice in 1969. His facility for executing simple, environmentally conscious forms within a modernist aesthetic can be best seen in understated houses such as Fredericks House (1982) in New South Wales and Marika-Alderton House in the Northern Territory. When Murcutt was awarded the Pritzker Architecture Prize in 2002, the jury cited his facility in manipulating building forms within a natural habitat, making structures that appear to float above the landscape.

This open-plan house has approximately 1,500 square feet (140 sq m). The house is constructed mostly of timber with steel and consists of prefabricated modules that were assembled on site. Its design focuses on operable walls and niches, and large roof eaves act as sunscreens. It has no glazing but instead uses sliding plywood panels. The house is raised above the ground to allow air circulation beneath and to protect it from animal intrusions and tidal surges during cyclones.

Vernacular buildings constructed using common materials are plentiful across the globe, but a few architects, such as Murcutt, have elevated these structures to a fine art. Similar works include those by U.S. architect Fay Jones and Swiss-born Peter Zumthor.

St. Benedict Chapel,
1988, Peter Zumthor
Sumvitg, Graubünden,
Switzerland

66

*Drawing with a pencil,
the hand can discover
the solution before the
mind can conceive it.*

?

Aboriginal artist Banduk Marika and her
partner Mark Alderton commissioned
Murcutt to create their house on the
north coast of Australia, Arnhemland, in 1991. It
would relate to its monsoonal tropical climate yet
be weather-tight and culturally responsible. Over the
next three years, the architect developed the design
of the house sympathetic to the landscape, hot
climate and Aboriginal traditions of the Yolnu People,
in the spirit of simplicity promoted in the writings of
Henry David Thoreau.

The cedar-frame construction is designed as garden structures within the woods, with an enclosed space that can be used for museum displays. This open-air plan allows the complex to be accessible to the public even when performances are not held.

NOH STAGE IN THE FOREST
KENGO KUMA
1996

Yokohama-born Kengo Kuma (1954–) studied at the University of Tokyo, graduating in 1979, and then at Columbia University under a fellowship from 1985 to 1986. He returned to Tokyo to open his own architectural practice in 1990 and continued to teach and study. His works eclectically combine traditional vernacular Japanese aesthetics with a contemporary mindset, creating very simple yet sometimes fragile, elegant architectural solutions attuned to both worlds. He uses natural materials in a way that makes buildings seem light, beautifully proportioned and serene. These include Bato Hiroshige Museum of Art (2000) in Tochigi, Japan, and the Great Bamboo Wall (2002) in Beijing, China. Kuma's Noh Stage in the Forest in Toyoma, Miyagi Prefecture, Japan, fits within this design philosophy. The architect's more recent works tend to look at dematerializing buildings further and treating them within a larger environment. Good examples are the shrine and adjacent apartment house for Akagi Jinja and Park Court Kagurazaka (2010) in Tokyo and Yusuhara Wooden Bridge Museum (2011), which connects two other buildings formerly separated by a roadway.

Well-known architects around the globe have been inspired by the vernacular, and their work bears comparison in terms of a combination of local yet modern forms. These include Fay Jones and Samuel Mockbee in the United States, Glenn Murcutt in Australia, and Peter Zumthor in Switzerland. As with that of many of these practitioners, Kuma's minimalism also relates to natural forms; he often compares his buildings to rainbows.

Kikatami Canal Museum, 1999, Kengo Kuma
Miyagi, Japan

FRAC (Regional Collection of Contemporary Art), 2013, Kengo Kuma
Marseille, France

Noh theatre traces its open-air performance style back to the 18th century. Kuma designed the complex as a living museum of Noh, complete with separate structures for stage and spectator space within a natural environment. This corresponds to the original intent of Noh theatre in Toyoma, where a bridge and a stage represent the two worlds of natural and supernatural, life and death.

It is my mission to use the kindness and delicacy that old architecture had. I believe that this mission is not easy . . . I am planning to work until I fall down.

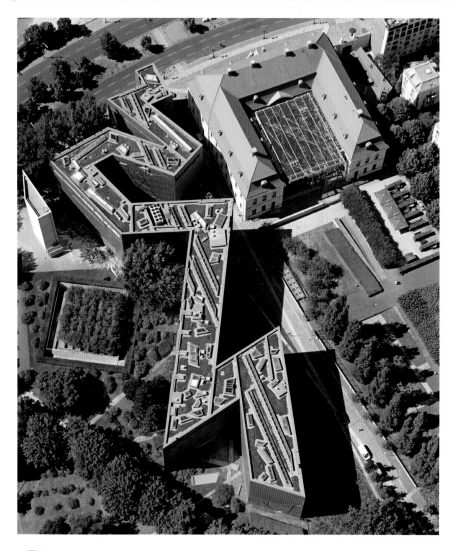

Libeskind conceived this distinctive form, with nonexhibit spaces or 'voids', in competition. The aggressive concrete interiors and lightning bolt exterior, as well as the unsettling navigation through angular forms, represent the disturbing experience of Jewish life in Berlin, and by extension all of Germany. Libeskind envisioned his design as the finale for Arnold Schoenberg's opera *Moses and Aron* (1932), in part because of the composer's exile from Berlin shortly before the Holocaust.

JEWISH MUSEUM
DANIEL LIBESKIND
2001

Polish-born U.S. architect Daniel Libeskind (1946–) was in the spotlight in 2003 for his World Trade Center reconstruction plan and the resultant controversy over the tower eventually built there. Although Libeskind has designed several high-rise complexes, such as Reflections (2011) at Keppel Bay, Singapore, and Haeundae Udong Hyundai I'Park (2012) in Busan, South Korea, he began his professional career on a different note. He trained initially in music in Israel and then architecture at Cooper Union in New York and Essex University in England. He first made his mark with two German buildings: the Jewish Museum in Berlin and the Felix Nussbaum House (1998) in Osnabrück. These institutions catapulted him to international recognition and led to other, mostly museum, commissions. These range from the Imperial War Museum North in Manchester (2001) and Contemporary Jewish Museum (2008) in San Francisco, to additions and renovations at Denver Art Museum (2006), Royal Ontario Museum (2007) and Military History Museum (2011) in Dresden. In his designs, Libeskind uses bold, slashing, angular forms to define a site presence, those forms shaping unique spatial experiences within. Since the Jewish Museum's opening in 2001 Libeskind has also made extensions to the complex in 2007, for a multiuse space and restaurant, as well as in 2012 for an archive.

The building is constructed of reinforced concrete with zinc cladding. Its dramatic lightning bolt design, often nicknamed 'blitz', houses a set of angular and rectangular galleries within, the entire building connected by passages. Some of these lead to views of bare concrete sharp-cornered voids. The largest one represents the Holocaust and the absence of Jewish contributions to Berlin's society. In order to experience the entire museum, visitors must cross this void, reminding them of society's loss.

"

The voids are 'that which can never be exhibited when it comes to Jewish Berlin history: humanity reduced to ashes'.

The first major museum devoted to the Holocaust was James Ingo Freed's United States Holocaust Memorial Museum (1993) in Washington, D.C. Libeskind's Jewish Museum tells its story with its design, not solely with the exhibition objects within.

United States Holocaust Memorial Museum, 1993, James Ingo Freed
Washington, D.C., USA

Illinois Holocaust Museum and Education Center, 2010, Tigerman McCurry
Skokie, IL, USA

City and state governments worked together to finance the $630 million renovation in order to keep the Chicago Bears football team in the city. Bears owner Michael McCaskey met architect Benjamin T. Wood in the late 1990s, asking his advice for a new stadium. Wood and Zapata was essentially responsible for the new design, which preserved the exterior of the original stadium but demolished the outdated and cramped interior. Although the overall capacity was reduced, the reconfiguration moved the spectators closer to the field of play.

I wouldn't do this if it were the Parthenon. But this isn't the Parthenon.

DIRK LOHAN

The reinforced-concrete shell was saved and a new, asymmetrically curved, steel-and-glass bowl inserted. The western side has open tiered seating and the eastern side enclosed luxury boxes. This made it one of the smallest stadia in the National Football League.

SOLDIER FIELD
WOOD AND ZAPATA
2003

After World War I, nations and cities erected memorials and commemorative buildings to honour their dead in the conflict that was supposed to be the war to end all wars. The Greek Revival Soldier Field (1924) in Chicago is one such memorial building. Designed in 1919 by Holabird and Roche with enormous Doric arcades, the stadium was officially dedicated on 27 November 1926, at the 29th Army–Navy American football game and has been the home of the Chicago Bears football team since 1971. In 2003 the renovation by Wood and Zapata, with Chicago-based Lohan Caprile Goettsch Associates, sparked a controversy that rumbles on today: journalists slammed it as an 'eyesore on Lake Shore' and 'acropolis meets apocalypse'. In 2006, it even lost its National Historic Landmark designation because of the radical renovation. Nevertheless, others have defended the space-age design in terms of upgrading the facility, keeping the team revenue in Chicago and providing improved parkland for the general public.

Olympic Stadium Renovation, 2004, Gerkan, Marg and Partners
Berlin, Germany

A *Spirit of the American Doughboy* statue by E.M. Viquesney was restored and installed here with the reopening in 2003.

It is difficult to bring historic stadia up to current expectations for fans and preservationists. A recent success is Gerkan, Marg and Partners' renovation in 2004 of Berlin's historic Olympic Stadium (1936).

Polshek's work has always been related to social service and the public sphere. He originally attended premed school before studying architecture and cites Quinco Regional Mental Health Center (1973) in Columbus, Indiana, as one of his favourite projects.

WILLIAM J. CLINTON PRESIDENTIAL CENTER
JAMES S. POLSHEK
2004

U.S. President Franklin D. Roosevelt began the tradition of presidential libraries by donating his to the U.S. government in 1941. The Presidential Libraries Act (1955) officially established this process, with libraries funded by private donations and then gifted to the federal government.

Some have become architectural monuments: I.M. Pei designed the John Fitzgerald Kennedy Presidential Library and Museum (1979) in Boston and Gordon Bunshaft was the architect for the Lyndon B. Johnson Presidential Library (1968) in Austin, Texas. Although Robert A.M. Stern's traditional George W. Bush Presidential Center (2013) in Dallas, Texas, is the most recent presidential building, perhaps a more architecturally adventurous one is the William J. Clinton Presidential Center in Little Rock, Arkansas, by James S. Polshek (1930–). The complex is located on the banks of the Arkansas River, and the main building is elevated above the riverbank. The Polshek Partnership has created some of the most important institutional buildings in the United States, including the Rose Center for Earth and Space at the American Museum of Natural History (2000) in New York City.

This aluminium-and-glass structure is sited dramatically 40 feet (12 m) above the Arkansas River within a remediated brownfield site, which incorporates historic structures such as Choctaw railway station (1901) and Rock Island Bridge (1899), converted to pedestrian use. Some 20,000 square feet (1,858 sq m) of museum exhibits are within the centre, which also houses a great hall for special events, an auditorium, a café and classrooms.

John F. Kennedy Presidential Library and Museum, 1979, I.M. Pei
Columbia Point, Boston, MA, USA

Polshek created a 24-foot (7-m) presentation drawing to help secure the commission for this prestigious library: a design presentation that not only referenced historic sites in Little Rock but also President Clinton's life there. The dramatically modern design contrasts with more predictable, conservative impressions of what an architect might create for a presidential library.

> *What I learned from [Louis Kahn] was modesty. Personal modesty—he never cared about publicity. And the modesty in the expression of the building.*

Military museums often incorporate memorials. Examples include fifty-two etched glass panels at Duxford that show the 7,031 U.S. planes and crew lost during World War II, and the curved memorial wall within the former USS *Intrepid*, illuminated with the names of 272 pilots and crew who died in service.

CANADIAN WAR MUSEUM

MORIYAMA & TESHIMA

2005

Raymond Moriyama (1929–) is one of Canada's classic modern architects. Vancouver-born of Japanese descent, he studied architecture and graduated from the University of Toronto (1954) and McGill University (1957), after earlier being detained as a youth in a Canadian internment camp for Japanese during World War II. He began his own practice in 1958, and his best-known early works are the blocky yet Asian-detailed Japanese Canadian Cultural Centre (1963)—a memorial to Canadians interned during the war—and the sleek, longitudinally concrete-and-glass Ontario Science Centre (1969), both in Toronto. In 1970 he joined in partnership with Ted Teshima (1938–). Their newer work, almost always of simple geometric forms in concrete or masonry, ranges from the Canadian Embassy (1991) in Tokyo to the Bata Shoe Museum (1995) in Toronto, and the National Museum of Saudi Arabia (1999) in Riyadh. One of their last works before retirement was the similarly massed, concrete Canadian War Museum in Ottawa, a project managed by design partner Diarmuid Nash. With Moriyama and Teshima both retired as emeritus partners, Nash, Moriyama's son Jason and Daniel Teramura continue the tradition of creating modern institutional buildings: among their newest works is Etihad Museum in the United Arab Emirates, under design in 2013 to 2015.

Three design options were prepared in 2002, with a budget of 102 million Canadian dollars. The design includes Canada's largest green roof and a low profile along the Ottawa River, which projects nature's regeneration of war-torn landscapes.

The architectural theme of the Canadian War Museum is regeneration, reflected in the building's sustainable design. Angled concrete walls give the visitor a sense of bunker-like unease, but perhaps the most powerful space within the museum is the chapel-like Memorial Hall. Canada's Unknown Soldier's tomb is installed there, illuminated by the sun at 11 a.m. each 11 November, Remembrance Day. Museum executives selected Moriyama's well-established firm in 2001 because of its proven track record regarding budgets and timely completion.

American Air Museum, 1997, Foster + Partners
Duxford, England

Renovation of the Intrepid Sea, Air and Space Museum, 2008, Eva Maddox and Ralph Johnson of Perkins and Will
New York, NY, USA

**HORNO 3
STEEL MUSEUM
NICHOLAS GRIMSHAW
2007**

Industrial archaeology blossomed in the 1970s and 1980s, laying the groundwork for major projects such as the Industrial Landscape Park (1991) at Duisburg-Nord, Germany. The park contains industrial ruins converted into cultural and recreational purposes, and it is one of 300 open-air projects built as part of a ten-year restructuring programme, begun in 1989, known as the International Building Exhibition. It received worldwide attention and led to other projects, such as Horno 3 Steel Museum (Blast Furnace 3) in Monterrey, Mexico. Of major contemporary architects, London-based Nicholas Grimshaw (1939–) is arguably the most attuned to industrial heritage. His designs honour buildings of the past, exemplified by his Waterloo International Terminal (1993) in London, where the steel detailing recalls the beauty of industrial-era fittings from the 1800s. Horno 3 was built originally in 1968 by Arthur G. McGee & Co., and functioned within the Fundidora Monterrey Iron and Steel Foundry until the works closed in 1986. This left it and the adjacent industrial land unused until the government of Nuevo León created a nonprofit foundation to develop the site for cultural purposes. With Horno 3 as its core, the new museum opened in 2007.

◿
In 2005 restoration began on this 262-foot-high (80-m) steel blast furnace, and it was designated a National Monument in 2009. A custom-built cab takes visitors to platforms some 137 feet (42 m) high, where they can meander among the various industrial forms. Grimshaw integrated sustainable features in exterior louvres, and cool air circulation at the lower level with hot air discharged above.

◎
Peter Latz's Landschaftspark (2002) is one of the oft-cited successes in repurposing a brownfield site into parkland, although earlier examples exist. These include Richard Haag's Gas Works Park (1978) in Seattle.

? Grimshaw created a dynamic adaptive reuse for this blast furnace as an interactive science centre, and it has had more than 800,000 visitors since its opening. He was selected for the project because of his sensitivity to great historic industrial forms and also for practical reasons. He had earlier designed the Hal 9000 Computer Centre (1999) for construction company supplier Cemex in Monterrey. The conversion probably led to other commissions, such as the Patricia and Phillip Frost Museum of Science in Miami, scheduled to open in 2015.

Deutsches Bergbau-Museum addition, 2009, Benthem Crouwel
Bochum, Germany

Rising stars Diller, Scofidio and Renfro were chosen because of the success of the Institute of Contemporary Art and other environmentally conscious works. According to the architects, the High Line was 'inspired by the melancholic unruly beauty of this postindustrial ruin, where nature has reclaimed a once vital piece of urban infrastructure'. Its success has influenced others to begin similar projects, such as Chicago's 606 park (2012) along the Bloomingdale freight line, designed by landscape architect Michael Van Valkenburgh.

Socrates Sculpture Park, 1986, Mark di Suvero Long Island City, New York, NY, USA

Olympic Sculpture Park, 2007, Weiss/Manfredi Seattle, WA, USA

HIGH LINE
DILLER, SCOFIDIO AND RENFRO
2009 & 2011

Diller, Scofidio and Renfro was founded by husband and wife team Ricardo Scofidio (1935–) and Elizabeth Diller (1954–), later joined by Charles Renfro (1964–). They established their reputation with the Institute of Contemporary Art (2001) in Boston, followed by the High Line in New York City, begun in 2006. Here, they were part of a team that converted a disused elevated freight railway (1934) on Manhattan's west side into an urban park. Their overall planning was detailed further by landscape architect James Corner Field Operations with planting by Piet Oudolf. The High Line's location just off the Hudson River makes it a tourist favourite that is used regularly by residents, too, and its success has impacted positively on property values and new construction, such as the Standard Hotel (2009) by Polshek Partnership. The project is an extension of the field of industrial archaeology first popularized in England and the United States in the 1970s. There are a number of similar projects that date back to that era in which disused industrial corridors became linear parks with hiking trails and bicycle pathways. Examples include London's Grand Surrey Canal System (1826), Chicago's Illinois and Michigan Canal (1848), and New York's Croton Aqueduct (1842).

The abandoned decaying steel-and-concrete structure 30 feet (9 m) above the street was first stabilized and restored, and wooden and concrete landscaping elements with wildflower plantings, water fountains, sun decks, viewing cutouts and benches were integrated with sections of original railway track along the 1.45-mile (2.3-km) length, which stretches from Gansevoort Street to 34th Street. New steel staircases and lifts provide access points from 30th to Gansevoort streets. The landscaped spaces are also used for public performances and art installations. Because of its location in midtown Manhattan, more than 3 million visitors use the park each year.

Besides having precedents in pathways atop 19th-century infrastructures, the High Line was probably influenced by Paris's Promenade Plantée (1993), designed by Philippe Mathieux and Jacques Vergely and built atop a disused rail line. Seattle's Olympic Sculpture Park (2007) also has its roots in industrial space and is a good comparison with the High Line in regard to its dynamic reuse of a large urban brownfield.

We're all about the public realm.
CHARLES RENFRO

FORTALEZA HALL
NORMAN FOSTER
2010

Temple of Dendur,
Metropolitan Museum
of Art, 1978,
Roche-Dinkeloo
New York, NY, USA

Liberty Bell Center, 2003,
Bohlin Cywinski Jackson
Philadelphia, PA, USA

It is a challenge to add to a major monument by a renowned architect, let alone create an important building nearby. English architect Norman Foster (1935–) succeeded in doing exactly that with Fortaleza Hall on the Johnson Wax corporate campus in Racine, Wisconsin. It is an architectural pilgrimage site dominated by Frank Lloyd Wright's National Historic Landmark: the Johnson Wax Administration Building (1939) and Johnson Wax Research Tower (1950). In contrast to some of Foster's spectacular steel-and-glass office buildings; dramatically modern steel, glass, and concrete airports; and low-lying spaceport, the design solution for Fortaleza Hall is an elegantly simple one. It recalls the spirit of exhibition pavilions past, and is comparable to the German Pavilion at Barcelona International Exposition (1929), designed by Ludwig Mies van der Rohe. Fortaleza Hall is named after a city in Brazil, where in 1935 a company expedition—in a Sikorsky S-38 amphibious airplane—led to the discovery of a natural wax source: the Carnaúba tree. The journey was re-created in 1998 in a replica airplane, which is showcased within Fortaleza Hall. The Community Building, which adjoins Fortaleza Hall, provides light, open space for employees compared with Wright's building in which the atrium space is inwardly focused.

A number of U.S. exhibition pavilions have been constructed to showcase only one object, such as the Vatican Pavilion (1964) at the New York World's Fair built for Michelangelo's *Pietà* (1498–1499). Enshrining a singular artefact within a tempietto goes back even further, to the McKim, Mead and White-designed temple for Plymouth Rock (1920) in Massachusetts.

The building incorporates a background soundtrack that replicates sounds of Brazil's atmosphere, with weather updates using data from the National Oceanic Atmospheric Administration.

A Royal Air Force veteran and accomplished pilot, Foster has been fascinated by airplanes since childhood. He was therefore the perfect choice for this 360-degree shrine to an airplane whose expedition was a major factor in the rise of Johnson Wax to become a global brand. The pavilion-like building displays the replica plane suspended from the ceiling as if in mid flight. In *Towards a New Architecture* (1923), Le Corbusier compared the Parthenon in Athens with a Caproni hydroplane, raising aviation to an art form; Foster cited this work as an architectural influence.

The pavilion is constructed of eighty-five ultra-clear, low-iron glass panels. It is partly encircled by a curved Kasota limestone structure compatible with the same design and materials used by Wright in Johnson's corporate buildings. Interior spaces house exhibits and also a range of amenities for employees, including a fitness centre, bank, shop and café.

Light it, open it up to a view.... For me, space is inseparable from light and shadow.

Piano's building is scaled equally to Kahn's with a 300-foot (91-m) facade housing galleries, an auditorium, a café, a shop and parking. Materials include a soft grey concrete and light-coloured Douglas fir beams. The complex is energy efficient, incorporating geothermal cooling and photovoltaic roof panels.

KIMBELL ART MUSEUM EXPANSION
RENZO PIANO
2013

Italian architect Renzo Piano (1937–) graduated from the Polytechnic University of Milan in 1964 and worked for Louis Kahn before creating his own firm: Renzo Piano Building Workshop. The practice achieved global recognition with awards such as the Pritzker Architecture Prize in 1998, and more recently has expanded to build major commercial structures such as The Shard (2012) in London. Earlier, however, Piano established a reputation for precisely designed and finely proportioned museum buildings, notably the Menil Collection (1987) and adjacent Cy Twombly Gallery (1995) in Houston. Later examples include Jean-Marie Tjibaou Cultural Centre (1998) in New Caledonia and Nasher Sculpture Center (2003) in Dallas, along with large additions to Pierpont Morgan Library (2006) in New York, the Art Institute of Chicago's Modern Wing (2009) and Boston's Isabella Stewart Gardner Museum (2012). With his expertise in restrained, modernist museum design, Piano was a natural choice to create an addition to the famed Kimbell Art Museum complex in Fort Worth, Texas—an architectural masterpiece built by Kahn four decades earlier.

It is a confident architect who can successfully add to a well-known building. Some additions are controversial, such as Soldier Field (2003) by Wood and Zapata; others are more respectful yet still project the architect's personality, such as the Visitor Center at Darwin D. Martin House (2008) by Toshiko Mori, an addition to a Frank Lloyd Wright-designed complex.

Modern Art Museum, 2002, Tadao Ando
Fort Worth, TX, USA

Visitor Center, Darwin D. Martin House, 2008, Toshiko Mori
Buffalo, NY, USA

? It is not easy to build next to a design landmark. Piano created a restrained, respectfully modernist design, distinct from Kahn's Kimbell building in materials and overall presentation yet comfortable beside it. Kahn's concrete volumes contrast with Piano's lightness in concrete, glass and wood, emphasized by design features such as a glazed skeletal roof that seemingly floats above the building. The lightness of Piano's spaces is made even lighter by the use of thin movable walls.

[The addition to the Kahn complex is] close enough for a conversation, not too close, and not too far away.

?

Unlike Predock's previous angular masonry forms, the curving, swooping design of steel and glass ascends from its historic limestone base in a swirling spiral. It was inspired by the Canadian landscape and responds to the archaeological importance of its site. According to the museum administration, the building is 'carved into the earth . . . dissolving into the sky' with 'the abstract, ephemeral wings of a white dove'.

CANADIAN MUSEUM FOR HUMAN RIGHTS

ANTOINE PREDOCK

2014

Albuquerque-based Antoine Predock (1936–) is well known for institutional buildings, ranging from his early work at the University of New Mexico Law School (1971) to the later Nelson Fine Arts Center (1989) at Arizona State University and Las Vegas Central Library and Children's Museum (1990). All share a commonality in terms of blocky, geometric masonry forms akin to the historic adobe thick-walled buildings of the American Southwest. Predock's work expanded to incorporate large entertainment venues such as Hotel Santa Fe at Euro Disney (1992) near Paris and Petco Park (2004) for the San Diego Padres baseball team. As part of his oeuvre, the architect created a series of museums beyond his usual practice in the Southwest. These include fine art spaces, such as Tang Teaching Museum (2000) in New York and Tacoma Art Museum (2003) in Washington, as well as science and nature centres, such as Flint RiverQuarium (2004) in Georgia and Trinity River Audubon Center (2008) in Dallas. They all display Predock's visual interest in bold geometric forms, often in concrete. However, the Audubon Center's curved shapes prefigure further explorations away from hard-angled geometry, seen in Winnipeg's Canadian Museum for Human Rights, with associate architects Smith Carter.

This structure has a Tyndall stone base that houses the great hall, intended to evoke gatherings of First Nation peoples at this site: excavations unearthed 400,000 artefacts from a millennium ago. Alabaster ramps lead to galleries, the Garden of Contemplation and the 328-foot (100-m) Tower of Hope.

National Underground Railroad Freedom Center, 2004, Boora Architects Cincinnati, OH, USA

[My buildings] are an accumulation of vantage points both perceptual and experiential.

Sites of Conscience is a global coalition of museums and historic sites, established to help create a more just and humane future. North American members include this new museum, the National Underground Railroad Freedom Center (2004) in Cincinnati and the National Civil Rights Museum (1991) in Memphis, site of the assassination of Martin Luther King Jr.

The museum was the first Canadian project to use a virtual design and construction program that linked architects, designers and contractors from Canada, the United States and Germany.

INDEX

Page numbers in **bold**
refer to illustrations

PICTURE CREDITS

2 Vladimir Sazonov/Shutterstock.com 8–9 © Prisma Bildagentur AG/Alamy 10 © Chicago Historical Society/Hedrich Blessing Archive/VIEW 12–13 © Condé Nast Archive/CORBIS 14–15 Adrián Mallol i Moretti/Flickr 16–17 © Robert Harding World Imagery/Alamy 18–19 © Vince Streano/CORBIS 20–21 Esparta Palma, www.esparta.co 22–23 Capitolshots Photography, capitolshots.com 25 Arnout Fonck/Flickr 26 photography Matthijs Borghgraef/Getty Images 28–29 © AGF Srl/Alamy 30–31 Scott Norsworthy 32–33 Walter Bibikow/Getty Images 34 Sira Anamwong/Shutterstock.com 36 © Prisma Bildagentur AG/Alamy 38–39 © epa european pressphoto agency b.v./Alamy 40 © Bill Brooks/Alamy 42–43 © Ekain Terroba 45 © Backyard Capture/Alamy 46 © Scott Norsworthy 48 © Emma Smales/VIEW 50–51 © Iwan Baan 52–53 © Arcaid Images/Alamy 55 Belgium, Brussels, Atomium/Getty Images. www.atomium.be - sabam 2014. 56–57 Steve Geer/Getty Images 58 © Brad Mitchell/Alamy 60–61 © Zoonar GmbH/Alamy 62–63 © Dennis MacDonald/Alamy 64–65 © Charles E. Rotkin/CORBIS 66–67 © Arcaid Images/Alamy 68–69 Sean Pavone/Shutterstock.com 70 © Paul Springett C/Alamy 72–73 © VIEW Pictures Ltd/Alamy © John Zukowsky 77 Vladimir Sazonov/Shutterstock.com 78–79 © Arcaid Images/Alamy 80–81 © Danita Delimont/Alamy 83 © VIEW Pictures Ltd/Alamy 84 © VIEW Pictures Ltd/Alamy 87 Alejandro Cartagena 88–89 © Christian Richters Photography 90–91 © Arcaid/Nigel Young/Foster + Partners 92–93 © Andre Jenny/Alamy 94–95 Eliot Elisofon/Contributor 96–97 © Everett Collection Historical/Alamy 98–99 © Bettmann/CORBIS 100–101 Guy Vanderelst 102–103 © Stanley Tigerman 104–105 © Danita Delimont/Alamy 106–107 Carol M. Highsmith's America, Library of Congress, Prints and Photographs Division. 108 Barry Winiker/Getty Images 110–111 © Everett Fanton Gidley 112–113 © Arcaid 2015/Alan Weintraub 114–115 © Fernando S. Gallegos. 116–117 © B Lawrence/Alamy 118–119 © Andre Jenny/Alamy 120–121 © Joachim S. Muller 122–123 © VIEW Pictures Ltd/Alamy 124–125 © John Zukowsky 126 American Spirit/Shutterstock.com 128–129 Eastimages/Shutterstock.com 130–131 © Efrain Padro/Alamy 132–133 Cultura Travel/Richard Seymour 135 © Bettmann/CORBIS 137 Raymond Boyd/Getty Images 138 © Massachusetts Institute of Technology Libraries, Visual Collections, Photograph by Peter Serenyi 140–141 © Jesus Gil/Demotix/Corbis 142–143 Kushch Dmitry/Shutterstock.com 144–145 © Duccio Malagamba 148 Fedor Selivanov/Shutterstock.com 151 © Diana Bier Torre Mayor/Alamy 152 © Lourens Smak/Alamy 154–155 © Göran Gustafson/Alamy 157 © Shin Takamatsu architect and associates Co., Ltd 158 © Richard Ellis/Alamy 160 © John Zukowsky 162 Bruno Morandi/Getty Images 165 Luciano Mortula/Shutterstock.com 166 Zhukov Oleg/Shutterstock.com 168–169 Eric Gregory Powell 170–171 Cultura Travel/Richard Seymour 172–173 © Archimage/Alamy 174–175 Amos Chapple 176–177 © Ian Dagnall/Alamy 178–179 © Philip Scalia/Alamy 180–181 © age fotostock Spain, S.L./Alamy 182–183 ©Katsuaki Furudate 184 Nagel Photography/Shutterstock.com 186–187 JMN/Getty Images 189 © Nabeel Turner 190 © mediacolor's/Alamy 192–193 © Chris Willson/Alamy 195 © Archimage/Alamy 196–197 Glenn Murcutt, courtesy Architecture Foundation Australia 198–199 © Kengo Kuma 200 Guenter Schneider 202–203 FeyginFoto/Shutterstock.com 204–205 © Douglas Keister/Corbis 206–207 © John Zukowsky 208–209 © Rivera/Archphoto: Paul/Arcaid/Corbis 210 Boston Globe/Contributor 212–213 © James Steinkamp Photography 214–215 © Nic Lehoux/VIEW/Corbis 216 © Ken Gillespie Photography/Alamy

p.2: Dancing House, Frank Gehry, Prague, Czech Republic

SOURCES

In terms of research, a vast quantity of information is available on the internet, and the field of architecture is no exception. The best sources are the websites of architects, national and regional architectural associations, organizations such as the Pritzker Architecture Prize, Driehaus Prize, and Council on Tall Buildings and Urban Habitat, as well as encyclopedias including Encyclopaedia Britannica and Wikipedia. Other excellent sources are online and print journals. *ArchDaily*, *Architectural Record*, and *The Architect's Newspaper* are but a few. Beyond these online sources, there is a host of architectural surveys and individual monographs, many of which are available in local libraries. Several include:

Mohammad al-Asad, *Mixed-Use Complexes: Constructing Icons*. Gainesville, FL: University Press of Florida, 2012.
Dennis P. Doordan, *Twentieth-Century Architecture*. New York: Harry N. Abrams, 2002.
Arthur Drexler, *Transformations in Modern Architecture*. New York: Museum of Modern Art, 1979.
Beth Dunlop, *Building a Dream: The Art of Disney Architecture*. New York: Harry N. Abrams, 1996.
Diane Ghirardo, *Architecture after Modernism*. London: Thames & Hudson, 1996.
Jonathan Glancey, *Modern Architecture*. London: Carlton Books, 2007.
Charles Jencks, *The Language of Postmodern Architecture*. New York: Rizzoli, 1977.
Philip Johnson and Mark Wigley, *Deconstructivist Architecture*. New York: Museum of Modern Art, 1988.
Denna Jones, ed. *Architecture: The Whole Story*. London: Thames & Hudson; New York: Prestel, 2014.
Christine Killory and René Davids, *Details in Contemporary Architecture*. New York: Princeton Architectural Press, 2007.
Kisho Kurokawa. *New Wave Japanese Architecture*. London: Academy Editions, 1993.
Paolo Portoghesi. *Postmodern*. New York: Rizzoli, 1983.
Alex Sánchez Vidiella, *The Sourcebook of Contemporary Architecture*. New York: Harper Design, 2011.
James Steele, *Architecture Today*. London: Phaidon, 1997.
Alexander Tzonis and Liane Lefaivre, *Architecture in Europe since 1968*. New York: Rizzoli, 1992.
Philip Wilkinson. *Great Buildings*. London: DK Publishing, 2012.

First published in the United Kingdom in 2015 by
Thames & Hudson Ltd, 181A High Holborn,
London WC1V 7QX

This book was designed and produced by
Quintessence Editions Ltd.
The Old Brewery, 6 Blundell Street,
London, N7 9BH

Editor	Becky Gee
Designer	Tom Howey
Editorial Assistant	Zoë Smith
Production Manager	Anna Pauletti
Editorial Director	Jane Laing
Publisher	Mark Fletcher

British Library Cataloguing-in-Publication Data
A catalogue record for this book is available from
the British Library

ISBN 978-0-500-29178-8

Printed in China

To find out about all our publications, please visit
www.thamesandhudson.com.
There you can subscribe to our e-newsletter, browse or download
our current catalogue, and buy any titles that are in print.